Frontiers of Social Anthropology

Samira Dasgupta
Amitabha Sarkar

GYAN

GYAN PUBLISHING HOUSE

New Delhi 110 002

Frontiers of Social Anthropology

(Anthropology, Tribal Studies, Sociology)

ISBN : 81-212-0528-X

Published in 1996 in India by
Gyan Publishing House
5 Ansari Road
New Delhi 110 002

Printed at Mehra Offset Press, New Delhi.

DEDICATED TO

Respected Shri Biswanath Banerjee
Reader, Dept. of Anthropology
Calcutta University.

And

Respected Dr. Biman K. Dasgupta
Deputy Director (Retd.) Anthropological
Survey of India, Calcutta.

CONTENTS

PREFACE

Anthropology means the science of man. Anthropology studies man holistically, that is, from the physical as well as socio-cultural angles. The present volume is a basic tool for the students of anthropology, especially social anthropology deals with aim and scope or the horizon of social anthropology with its methodology. The scope of social anthropology extends from the primitive phase of man to contemporary developments in human society and their problems. The basic unit of observation for a social anthropologist is group behaviour which starts from the family. The theoretical part and application of anthropological knowledge in the field primarily depend on intensive fieldwork which serves as the laboratory for an anthropologist. The application of anthropological knowledge in the various socio-cultural situations is often found helpful even in developmental programmes, for which the anthropologist may be called as the social doctor.

In connection with the writing of the present study, the authors are indebted to Sri Biswanath Banerjee, Reader, Department of Anthropology, Calcutta University for his valuable suggestions and Kumari Shanta Bala of Jagdalpur, for her neat typing work.

Samira Dasgupta
Amitabha Sarkar

Calcutta (West Bengal)

1 Aim and Scope of Anthropology

One of the still unresolved theoretical problems engaging the attention of anthropologists is where to put the anthropology among the physical sciences, among the biological and natural sciences, or among the social sciences and humanities.

As we know that anthropology studies man—both from his physical as well as from the cultural point of view. So the study of former type is directly related to biological and natural sciences, and the study of the latter type is intimately related to natural and social sciences. As the study of man provides us a vast field, the anthropologists have to follow the methods of other allied sciences to solve their problems wherever necessary.

So we can say that anthropology is a complex science, as the subject is regarded as the science of all other sciences.

CULTURAL ANTHROPOLOGY

Aim, Scope and Relation to other Disciplines

Cultural anthropology is the main part of anthropology in which the human culture is studied.

It has taken all the branches of anthropology except those which are more concerned with the human biology.

Culture refers to the main behavioural characteristics of the human species. Culture is all that a man thinks and learns to do as a member of society. Man's culture is expressed in three levels like material pursuits which may be directly observed and handled, social activities—groupings and interrelations supported by marriage and kinship, etc., which can also be observed, and religious concepts that deals with supernatural aspects. It has to be kept in mind that man lives in society, as such his culture reflects in the background of his society or vice versa. The society means the totality of social facts projected on the dimension of groupings and relationships, culture is the totality in the dimension of actions. This suggests that there is an intimate relationship between society and culture, each of which cannot exist without the other. In this regard, it is better to call the man as a socio-cultural animal; so the term socio-cultural anthropology is more fruitful than the term cultural anthropology.

As we know that throughout the world, the people belong to various societies, and each of which remains developed and function in the background of their own culture. So the aim of social-cultural anthropology is to study the similarities and differences in social-cultural behaviour among different groups of people. It takes in all of the human social-cultural behaviour from the earliest beginnings of man's career to the great moment of present time. Cultural anthropologists study all the society and culture, whether carried on the tribal societies or in complex civilised nations. All aspects of culture including the technical and economic means of handling are considered. With the environment, i.e., material aspects, the way of relating or relationship to other people, i.e., social aspects, and the special experiences of religion and art, not only those activities within several aspects are studied, but the interplay among them is highlighted as the human culture is an integrated system. All these suggest that for the proper understanding of a particular culture and society, it is essential to take the multiple aspects with respect to their associated traits like—social, economic, political, language and education, religion, personality, etc., which are technically termed as social anthropology, economic anthropology, political anthropology, linguistic anthropology, psychological anthropology, and the anthropology of thought and religion.

Given the scope, the basic methods of cultural anthropology entails — (1) field study (2) holistic approach (3) comparative analysis and (4) generalisation and theorising from the empirical reality.

Thus the socio-cultural anthropology is a scientific discipline, as its generalisation is based on the controlled comparison which includes the co-ordination of induction and deduction.

The subject matter of socio-cultural anthropology (institutions and groupings) in most parts of the country functionally depend on or related to each other. The aim of science however, is to find out and explain their meaning and nexus. Our object of study is the human behaviour in the background of his culture and society. The unit here is the behaviour of a group of man. So the problem arises in which science it is to be placed and what its relation towards other disciplines?

Based on its aims and scopes, it is to be placed within the perimeters of social science. From the survey of available writings of the earlier anthropologists, it is rather evident that they were not bothered about this problem. Evolutionary and diffusionary interests serve as the sufficient levels for the study and the study is to be called as a natural science. The cultural anthropologists have also made use of models, like functional models (Brown, Malinowski, Nadel, and Fortes et al.,) drawn from natural science. But they drew the inspiration from the models of history and aesthetics (Kroeber, Prictchard, Benedict, Bidney, et al.,). In writing about the American anthropologists, Redfield believes that the future of anthropology should be characterised by a closer relationship with the humanities because of common interest. We think the holistic tendencies (i.e., studying the culture in its totality, the study of man at all levels of culture, and developing interests in the personality and values) of cultural anthropology gives us a scope to take the help drawn by natural sciences, social sciences and as well as the humanities to some extent.

Historical Background and Recent Development

Right from the beginning, the cultural anthropologists were faced with problems of the growth of a culture and cultural parallels, i.e., how do culture comes to be and how they come to have similar culture traits and complexes? The earlier studies were concerned with these problems.

Darwin published the *Origins of Species* (1859), in which he showed that man has evolved from the unicellular organism to this complex multicellular organism, through the process of evolution. This may be said to the date of birth of anthropology as also of the evolutionary studies. Being influenced by the Darwin's idea, a group of intellectuals like Spencer, Morgan, Tylor, et al., worked independently and deduced that evolution had not only operated in the case of the physical aspects of mankind, but in the cultural values of life. According to them the contemporary human culture is the results of evolution. Thus, multiple cultures were supposed to grow through evolution from simpler to complex and differentiated types. This is known as the evolutionary theory in cultural anthropology. The opinion of the evolutionist are:

> The culture is evolved and grown as the process of evolution from time after time. Based on this idea, they had given emphasis on the study of history and development of the society from primitive to contemporary man, and for that they arranged the types and forms of society without any reference of time and space. For these objectives, they have collected the facts from the contemporary primitive peoples.

After this phase, another group of intellectuals later denied the theory of evolution and postulated a contradiction the *theory of culture diffusion.*According to them, the instances of evolutionist that the culture traits always evolve independently and the culture similarities are the consequence of parallel or convergent evolution is not fully true. Diffusionists believe that culture growth and culture parallels were the result of diffusion, i.e., transmission of culture from one place to another. The founder of diffusionist theory are Ratzel, Graebner, Elliot Smith, Perry, Boas, Kroeber, Wiser, Benedict et al. The opinion of the diffusionists are as follows:

1. Culture grows at different regions according to its need and
2. Culture grows and changes due to contact or diffusion or borrowing of other cultures.

Whereas the characteristic features of diffusionist are:

1. Study of history.
2. Study of ecology or environment.
3. Study of culture contact or acculturation.

Infact, the evolutionists did not consider time and space in arranging types and forms of society towards advancement, which was explained by the diffusionists through migration.

In their view, both the evolutionists and the diffusionists differ in their opinion, but agreed in at least two points. They resemble each other. These are : (i) both explained the present civilisation in the context of the past and (ii) both of them made the subject as history. Their study began from the primitive society and ended into the contemporary one. Their study is based on "How we have become civilised"? It has nothing to do with the contemporary one. So the aim and scope of the cultural anthropology is not fulfilled by these studies, as these are eventually a historical account, which has nothing to deal with the science of society.

After getting some satisfactory answer on the problem of culture growth and parallelism some intellectuals however have raised the question "what is the internal structure of culture? How does it exist and function? In this connection Durkheim, Brown and Malinowski put forward their view points which was known as functionalism. They held that there is an inner consistency of a culture, or in other words culture is an integrated whole. The more important effect of functionalist is the emergence of the concept or integration in a culture, the inter-connectedness of traits in their webs of functions and meanings.

Structuralists and functionalists are of the opinion that:

1. study of culture should begin from the present condition without any reference to past as there is no concrete history available.

2. for better understanding the study should be compared with the other.

The views of Brown and Malinowski turned many anthropologists from their earlier concentration of historical studies to a new interest in examining the nature and function of contemporary culture and society. The functionalists insist in the interrelatedness or interconnectedness of things (holistic), solely responsible for the comprehensive and detailed professional field studies, which were unknown to the anthropologists of the nineteenth century. The present day anthropologists seem more clear in their perception than their predecessors that an understanding of culture is viewed in its full social setting. So, through the efforts of functionalist, the social-cultural anthropology became a scientific discipline, which deals with the structure and function of human culture (society), which is indispensible to the human beings for their survival. Till today, the social-cultural anthropologists depend basically on functional approaches of the study, though this method of study varies from one to another. Functionalists approach of interconnectedness of traits in a culture leads the subject for its further development into several sub-sections like; economic anthropology deals mainly with the economic activities of a culture and society; political anthropology deals mainly with the political and administrative aspects in terms of social control; social anthropology on the social facts of a society and culture, linguistic anthropology attempts on the language and educational aspects of the society and culture;

psychological anthropology about the cultural personalities of a society and lastly the anthropological studies of a religion of a society accounts for the supernatural aspects of the society and culture.

From Primitive Society to Civilised Nation

The name of anthropology suggests that it is the study of man without the limitation of time, place and cultural level. Then the question arises, why the cultural anthropologists study only the primitive society? This has been the consequence of historical accident, and later on, also of deliberate choice.

Being influenced by the Darwinian principles of evolution, the early explorers, travellers, and administrators of the eighteenth and nineteenth centuries studied the primitive societies for any evidence that might help in assimilating facts about the origin of human institutions. The diffusionists have a notion to trace the diffusion of culture traits (basically the material one) from the isolated primitive societies. Though in the twentieth century, the evolutionary bias has lost its appeal, the anthropologists of functional interpretation had studied the primitive isolates. In 1923, in a presidential address, Brown defined social-anthropology as the studies about the non-civilised people.

By definition, on the theoretical level, anthropology is often not confined to primitive society only. But in practice, excepting some very recent trends in research, the anthropologists have studied about the primitive societies only. The reasons behind this choice may be divided into conceptual and methodological ones. It is to be noticed that if we have two variant types of the same object of study, and one of which is simple and the other is complex, then the study of simpler type is useful in providing some methodological tools for the study of complex types. The simpler society or primitive society arises out of its being territorially limited, smaller population, racially and culturally homogeneous. One of the qualities of a simple society is its inner independence. Therefore, it is more convenient to fashion the tools of study on the primitive society, and with due modifications apply them to the more complex urban society. Ultimately, one has studied primitive society, it should be possible to acquire a fair idea of what the nature of human society (culture) is and this is what an anthropologist does. This kind of approach has been called microcosmic study by Firth—the study of macrocosm (the bigger unit) through the study of the microcosm (smaller unit). This is what is meant by Kluckhohn when he says studying the primitive society enables us to understood ourselves better. Evans Pritchard says that anthropologists must have studied primitive societies for their own sake, because they have an intrinsic value.

With the passage of time, the primitive societies got decimated. It is the fact that contact between primitive areas and modern people have resulted in certain changes. As a consequence, the primitive society (culture) is changed and being assimilated into non-tribal rural and urban societies. However, in this changed scenario, the anthropologists have faced crisis. To meet this challenge of the vanishing of their traditional material, anthropologists have widened their interests by approaching the community studies. In 1944, Brown said that social anthropology "has for its field all human societies". Lloyd Warner claimed all kinds of human societies—primitive or civilised, simple or complex, as the anthropological subject matter by studying the extremely primitive and extremely civilised aspects. Being influenced by this notion, the American anthropologists have moved in very rapidly to accept a part of the responsibility for studying civilised people, national status and such events as industrialisation and urbanisation. Today, it is useful for an anthropologist to study a community connected with or forming part of any civilisation or national status. The fact is that anthropologists have cognised the real small communities as parts of a larger and compound societal and cultural whole. The followers of this approach are Redfield, Singer, Cohn, *et al.*

New endeavours should be devoted to empirical researches, so that the validity of these concepts may be tested. At the present moment, the anthropologists are studying the human societies with respect to the magnitude of innate practical problems countered. Ginsberg (1939) had sorted out the problems in the following order :

(a) *Social Anthropology* : which includes the investigations of quality and quantity or the population inso far as they effect social relations and character of social groups, the study of social structure—the description and classification of principal types of social groups and institutions.

(b) *Social Control* about the study of law, moral values, religion and other regulating agencies of society and culture.

(c) *Social Process* : The study of various modes of interaction between the individuals or groups including co-operation and conflict, social differentiation and integration, change, development and decay.

(d) *Social Pathology* : The study of social maladjustment on the methodology used for dealing with them.

Each of the above mentioned problems is intrinsically related to one another, for proper understanding of a society (culture) all the problems are taken into account, as the culture is an integrated whole. An easier study calls into a population problem, but the relation to other is drawn as reference to the particular.

The scope or horizon of anthropological study is increasing day by day in relation to their immediate societal problems, namely, industrialisation, cultural ecology, linguistic anthropology, social pathology or criminology, ethnicity, etc. Apart from these, the current trend is a methodological issue of understanding the socio-cultural problems through the inside-out approach or interpretive anthropology. In the following lines, the horizons of such studies are discussed.

(a) Industrialisation

About four decades ago, there was little scholarly interest to study the social transformation going on in the economically underdeveloped or newly developing areas. Some anthropologists were turning their attention for the observation of such system under various kinds of external impacts like industrialisation and urbanisation. Anthropologists like Beals have interpreted such concept earlier. Since then the study of industrialisation as the process of culture change has been accounted for in Anthropology.

Industrialisation means the process of adaptation in industry. Industry requires huge power-driven machines which work under overall human supervision. Such a mechanised industrialisation opens ample possibilities of massive employment for mass production. Thus industrialisation has been the new area of anthropological investigation, especially in the underdeveloped countries where people move from simpler peasant economy to higher complex economy. Due to this, the problem faced by them in their daily lives eventually become the area of enquiry. Again in modern world industrialisation or changes in production embraces all sorts of changes in human life. Thus the industry is like the centre of a web, whose strands reach out to embrace almost every aspect of society, culture and personality.

So to an anthropologist, the study of industrialisation and its impact on society and culture is very much important to know how the changes recur in a particular culture on one hand, and its mode of adjustment on the other. The most concrete form of study of industrialisation, is to select an area where the factory is located and to investigate the life of the people of the area, as well as the workers employed in the industry. This type of study was attempted by Manning Nash (1958) among the Indian society of Guatemala, which is followed by Orans (1958), Moore (1963), Hoslitz (1963), Lambert (1963), Das and Banerjee (1962), Vidyarthi (1970), Singer (1972), Dasgupta (1978), Banerjee (1981), Dasgupta (1986), Sarkar (1988,1989,1990 and 1993).

(b) Cultural Ecology

The social-cultural anthropologists of present era think that cultural ecological approach is fruitful to understand man, his society and culture. Cultural ecology points that there is an intimate relationship between a culture and its surrounding environment. The total environment is inclusive of both the controlled and uncontrolled environment. Man has control over one environment, while a part of that not amenable to his control—called the uncontrolled environment is otherwise known as geographical environment to which man tries to adapt and adjust. The controlled environment is otherwise known as the social environment. In fact, the environment is the sum total of the social and geographical environments.

According to Sahlin (1964), cultures are human adaptation. Human beings have sufficient capacity to adapt the ecology for the sake of their existence. The cultural ecologists search for the adaptation of societies to specify environment. As the first exponent of cultural ecology, Steward (1955) eliminates biological ecology from its orbit, though A. Vayda, Roy. Rappaport, Robin Fox (1970) spoke for an important place for biological ecology in the study of cultural ecology. There is a causal connection between culture and environment. Steward feels that cultural-ecological adaptations are responsible for distinctive cultural traditions. Even the functioning of a culture is considered by the local environmental conditions. The culture determinism of Marvin Harris (1966) also involves technology, economy and natural environment. For Steward, the study of cultural ecology should take note of interrelationship between the behaviour pattern and productive technology and a very closely related aspect to observe how the behavioural pattern affects other spheres of culture. Hence there is dialectic interplay between the culture and environment.

The origin of particular cultural features or structures could also be known by analysing socio-cultural environmental adaptation. There are various conceptual approaches to understand human ecology which are as follows :

(i) *Environmental determinism.* In this concept, it is said that environment of a particular area determines its culture directly. The founder of this concept are Ratzel, Sempel (1911), et al.

(ii) *Environmental possibilism.* Environmental possibilism mentions that environment limits the possibilities of cultural development but not directly determines the culture of a particular area. A.L. Kroeber, Toynbee (1947) and Forde (1934) are the believers of this concept.

(iii) *The concept of cultural ecology.* The founder of the concept is Steward (1955). Ecological Anthropology emerged from Boasian School of historical particularism (diffusion). According to Steward, the interaction between the environment and the technology is related with the core of culture which includes the population structure, economy and the socio-political structure. He ignored the important part of human behaviour that is ideology. Before Steward, all the scientists used to limit their concept on the material culture. Greetz (1963) and Harris (1966) also followed the model of cultural ecology propounded by Steward.

(iv) *Eco-system based model.* A.Vayda (1968 and 1969), Rappaport (1968) suggested that instead of studying how cultures are adapted to the environment, attention should be focussed on the relationship of specific human population to specific eco-system. In their view, the human beings constitute simply another population among the many varieties of plants and animal species that interact with one another and with the non-living components (climate, soil, water) of their local eco-system. Thus the eco-system rather than culture, constitutes the fundamental unit of analysis in their conceptual framework for human ecology.

(v) *The actor-based model.* The adaptation occurs

primarily at the level of individual rather than at the level of group, population and social system. The founder of the model is Benjamin Orlov (1980). This model emphasised the process by which the people make decision in order to interact with their environment.

(vi) *Systems model.* A major scientific development in recent years has been the formulation of *general systems theory*, which is concerned with the general properties of the structures and functions of systems rather to their specific contents, viz., adaptation and selection through interaction between the eco-systems and social systems [Greetz (1963), Rambo (1983)]. Eco-system includes water, soil, climate, flora and fauna, i.e., fish, pet livestock, crops, trees, etc., and social system includes the social organisation, nutrition, health, population, technology, economy, religious values, language, etc. In the systems model of human ecology, both the social system and the eco-system with which it interacts retain their integrity as systems, each changing its structural configuration according to the internal dynamics.

(c) Linguistic Anthropology

Transmission of behaviour by learning from one generation to another is known as the culture. Social learning is found among the animals but the absence of speech among them limits the amount of acquisition. Man alone has such acquisition. Language is the vehicle by which culture is transmitted. Culture can accumulate little by way of knowledge and technology, but the former becomes civilisation only when written language comes into existence.

The anthropologists are of the opinion that language grows up in correlation with culture. Speech is a biological factor that is innate but a language is an acquired character. The geographic or climatic environment of which the languages are the product is not a natural one but social.

Hymes has defined the linguistic anthropology as the study of speech and language. So also Mandelbaum has said, "in linguistic anthropology, the students find striking demonstration of underlying patterns in a culture, of order, neatness and predictability".

Hymes and Lounsbury have shown the technique in which linguistic anthropology has enhanced the study of language in the context of cultural environment and social use of language forms. The notion of primitive languages leads to the question of evolution and typology. Linguistic approach as an aid to anthropology may be regarded from many points. To the evolutionist, any language forms one of the tests which divides the man from the anthropoid apes. The sociologists correlate the phonetic system with the structure of the organs connected with the mechanism of speech. The ethnologist studies the language for the evidence of ethnic identity or social contact or as a method to determine the grade of culture of a people or as a reflection of their character. In 1847, Baron Bunsen showed that the whole of mankind could be classified according to the patterns of language. Mention can be made of the linguistic classification of Gallatin, Humboldt and Muller. Grierson first classified the Indian languages in five types, viz., Austro-Asiatic, Tibeto-Burman, Dravidian, Aryan and the unclassified.

Linguistic change is an index of cultural change. Language adapts, evolves and encounters the evolutionary competition—both as to the contents (specially vocabulary and syntactical usage) and as to the range of function it senses. The anthropologist's concern with the language as a part of the culture or with the learning a language as a tool for cultural investigation requires careful semantic description. Anthropology is more concerned with nationalities than with nation, with ethnic than with political grouping, but in nationalities and ethnic units, language is always a factor and often the basic one.

The transmission of culture and day-to-day co-operation upon which man depends for his livelihood and welfare would not have been possible without some organised system of communication. This need for communication is satisfied by man's power of speech, organised in the form of language and also by other forms of cultural symbolism. Thus, communication can be set in among the human beings by cultural responses what Piddington has termed it as the language. In short, the language is a cultural response of man.

(d) Social Pathology or Criminology

Man is a social animal and lives in a society. So a society is made up of two factors—an aggregate of individuals and a permanent organisation of their action and interaction. These gradually lead to sudden changes.

A society is dynamic in nature. Every society is changing either slowly or rapidly. In a rapidly changing society, the established relationships are disrupted, the harmony between social groups is destroyed and the individual members of the society suffer from confusion and emotional strain. In course of time, however, some of the changes are possibly assimilated, whereas others are not. Failure in the assimilation of such changes is due to the failure to adapt the new standards of values, customs, and ideologies. This leads to the maladjustment in the interactions between the individuals or groups or institutions. Social equilibrium is disturbed inviting the social disintegration. This is known as *Social Pathology.*

Social disorganisation or disequilibrium—what is called as social pathology is caused by two types of maladjustments—personal and cultural.

Personal maladjustment is caused by lack of ability among the individuals to keep pace with the changing ideals and institutions. The imbeciles and the handicapped like the deaf, blind, etc., may somehow or other adjust themselves in a simple rural sector where there is *mechanical solidarity* is found while it is completely absent in a complex competitive society environs in a city of *organic solidarity.*

There is another sphere where personal maladjustment occurs. The individuals of a society do not find suitable opportunity to satisfy their individual desires for playing a role and enjoying a status. The dissatisfied, consequently are either gradually eliminated or adjusted or satisfy themselves by an escape-mechanism such as day-dreaming and fantasy, wherein on an unreal of their own creation they will get their desires satisfied or organise or join smaller groups—the patterns of such behaviour is better suited to their inherent capacities. The latter group forms the gangs of juvenile or adult criminals, reactionary or groups of chronic dependents. They fail to respond in their cooperative lives and prove a burden upon the group or virtual manace to its persons and properties. To study the groups of juvenile or criminals are otherwise known as *criminology.*

Cultural maladjustment consists of disturbances in the adjustment between various parts of society and between individuals and the whole cultural complex.

From the legal point of view, crime is an offence against the law or land. In early society, crime in a legal sense was unknown. The sharp distinction between immoral acts, injurious acts, and criminal acts are the products of civilisation. In English common law the distinction between a criminal and a delinquent rests upon the difference of age. A child below the age of seven is regarded as incapable of committing any crime as the responsibility of an act depends on the capacity to distinguish between the right and the wrong. Therefore, the criminal is generally an adult above the age of sixteen while between seven and sixteen he is a delinquent. So according to the legal point, a criminal is punished while a delinquent is taken in charge by the court for his protection. But this legal criterion of age in the distinction between the criminal and delinquent is no longer held to be valid in social science. From the sociological point of view, either a criminal or a juvenile delinquent is one who is guilty of an act believed by a group that has the power to enforce its belief to be harmful to society and therefore prohibited. So crime depends on the culture pattern of the society to which the criminal belongs. The nature of punishment is also in consonance with the cultural configuration.

Society has through the ages dealt with the problems of crime and delinquency. In the past punishment was regarded as the only treatment which the delinquent and the criminal deserved. Fortunately, there is a change in this attitude in the recent past. The criminal law first took off its hands from the child. Then the delinquent was separated from the criminal on the basis of age and a different attitude, that a correction and reclamation has been prescribed for them.

The efforts by social anthropologists are to inculcate the same notion for the criminals. One of the outstanding examples in recent years at Tihar Jail, Delhi where Kiran Bedi—a woman I.P.S. officer tried to rehabilitate the prisoners in different ways of life, which is a kind of reformation among the patterns of behaviour of the prisoners. This approach was highly appreciated by many corners. In fact there is a word that it is better to hate the crime rather the criminals.

(e) Study of Ethnicity

Study of ethnicity is a new dimension in social-cultural anthropology. The word ethnic signifies, "a group with a common cultural tradition and a sense of identity which exists as a sub-group of a larger society; the members of an ethnic group differ with regard to certain cultural characteristics from the other members of their society" (Theodorson and Theodorson, 1969) while the term ethnicity is a social group which consciously shares some aspects of a common culture and is defined primarily by descent or inheritance.

Study of ethnicity from socio-cultural point of view is an important domain to understand the ethnic demography, ethnic division of labour, dual labour market, who are the sons of soil, rise of nativism, problem of citizenship, etc. For the last couple of years, there are several ethnic unrest prevailed in various pockets of our country. These created a tension in a peaceful environment of our country. To eradicate, this study of ethnicity is essential to understand the root of the problem, calling for the recognition of services of anthropologists.

(f) Inside-out Approach (Interpretive Anthropology)

For explanation and diagnosis, the socio-cultural anthropology depends mainly on comparison, or analytic procedures. In case of ethnographic approach, the method is deductive or "outside-in" or "centripetal". If the analysis starts from the individual or family or domestic units and extends to find out its relation with all other institutions namely, economics, political, supernatural, etc., the method is inductive or 'inside-out' or centrifugal. Any way, the socio-cultural anthropology is a science as its generalisation is based on 'controlled comparison' which includes co-ordination of induction as well as deduction. The notable studies in this arena are *Rensangirri* of R. Burling, *Five Families* of Oscar Lewis, *Family Web* of Sarah Hobson, etc.

In short, "Interpretive anthropology is a covering label for a diverse set of reflections upon both the practise of ethnography and the concept of culture. It grew out of the confluence in the 1960s and 1970s of ideas from the then dominant version of social theory—the sociology of Talcott Parsons, from classic Weberian sociology, and from the simultaneous impact of a number of philosophical and intellectual fashions, including phenomenology, structuralism, structural and transformational linguistics, semiotics, Frankfurt school critical theory, and hermeneutics. These theoretical resources provided the elements for the appearance of unprecedentedly sophisticated discussion concerning the primary aspiration of ethnography, present from its modern inception, to elicit the native point of view and to elucidate how different cultural constructions of reality affect social action" (Marcus and Fischer, 1986).

"Interpretive anthropology operates on two levels simultaneously" it provides accounts of other worlds from the inside, and reflects about the epistemological grounding of such accounts" (Marcus and Fischer, 1986).

"Commentary on developments in anthropological thought during these two decades has tended to focus on the shift in stress from behaviour and social structure, undergirded by the goal of a natural science of society, to meaning, symbols and language and to a renewed recognition, central to the human sciences, that social life must fundamentally be conceived as the negotiation of meanings. Interpretive anthropology thus gives priority to the study of the *messier* side of social action, which had been relegated to marginal status in perspectives that instead emphasized the study of behaviour, objectively measured and assessed by the detached scientist. However, commentaries on the emergence of interpretive anthropology have given less attention to how, almost without being noticed, the affort to conceive of culture primarily as systems of meaning has come to focus on the process of interpretation itself, that is, on ethnography as a process of knowledge. The metaphor of cultures as texts, popularized by Greetz (1973), served to mark vividly the difference between the behavioural scientist and the cultural interpreter. According to this view, social activities can be 'read' for their meanings by the observer just as written and spoken materials more conventionally are. What's more not only the ethnographer reads symbols in action, but so do the observed—the actors in relation to one another. The critical question is what this evocative metaphor of interpretation as the reading of texts both by the observer and the observed stands for in the actual process of research. This has led to the present dominant interest within interpretive anthropology about how interpretations are constructed by the anthropologist, who works in turn from the interpretations of his informants. The attraction of interpretive anthropology at the moment is precisely its sophisticated inquiry into the nature of ethnographic reporting, which is not only the basis of all anthropological knowledge, pursued in whatever theoretical direction, but also one palatable predicaments, stimulated by the contemporary crisis of representation; historically anthropology has been near to them in institutional definition as a social science, but far in the singularity of its subject and method". (Marcus and Fischer 1986).

2 Family, Marriage and Kinship

The family is the smallest social group, usually composed of a father, a mother and one or more dependent children, in which the affection and responsibility are equally shared and the children are reared to become self-controlled and socially motivated persons. The basic psycho-social element in the family is the fellowship which comes from the sharing of problems by parents and the children in mutual respect and love. According to Murdock (1949), the family is a social grouping characterised by common residence, economic cooperation and reproduction. While the opinion of MacIver and Page about family—a grouping defined and enduring to provide for the creation and upbringing of children.

For proper rearing up of a child, an organisation is essential. By marriage, the individuals of opposite sexes come in closeness and the biological relationship gets established. The husband, the wife and the children borne out of that biological union forms groups with a bondage of blood relation. This ultimately gives rise to a comparatively stable group with traits like care, affection and discipline. This group is almost universal in its distribution. The term 'family' is widely used to denote such groups.

Existence of a marriage bond—present or past between the two or more members of the group is the main characteristic feature. This bond is sometimes broken by divorce, but always by death. In polygamous and extended families there is simultaneous marriage ties between more than two members. This bond is absent in consanguine family of the Nayars of Malabar. Family to the sociologist is the smallest social group based on marriage and kinship. Domestic and household units are also included in the modern classification of family.

Every social group have some specific forms, features and function by which it can work and when all these conditions fulfil, we may label this unit as a 'family'.

Forms

Man is a social being. He always wants to live in a social unit. The simplest form of social unit based on marriage is family. A family consists of parents and their offspring. But the unit though dependent on marriage should not always be understood in a biological sense. Among the Todas of Nilgiri hills, the consideration of biological fatherhood may depend upon a mere social ceremony. In the case of an adopted son among the Hindus (known as *Dattak putra*) social function is an essential part in claiming a father. Hence family though based on marriage should be considered as a social rather than a biological unit.

As a social unit, the family may be either unilateral or bilateral. In unilateral cases, the relations may be either paternal or maternal. The modern cases in civilised societies are usually paternal. A family through female relations is to be found among the Khasis of Meghalaya and the Nayars of South India. The bilateral family where the relations of both the parents, i.e., father and mother, come to live together is comparatively rare. This is, however, may be labelled as a kindred grouping. The best example is to be found among the Tavity of Eddystone islands in Western Solomon. The different forms or types of families are :

(a) When a person belongs to his family and his origin, it is known as *family of orientation.*

(b) When a person after marriage creates a family of its own it is known as *family of procreation.*

Simple or monogamous family : It is based on monogamy, i.e., marriage between a man and a woman. This family is the simplest of all. It is composed of parents and their unmarried children. It is also known as "biological" or "nuclear" family.

Joint or extended family : A joint family is a uniform unit of more than one family, having a common mess, a common habit at and a joint form of worship. The Hindu joint family is the most typical form of this kind. In these cases, a common hearth is found mainly among Bengalis. A Hindu joint family has a *karta* (Head), who looks after the actual management of the family affairs. He is always an elderly male most suitable by age and experience, and enjoys a mutual respect of other members of the family. The joint family may be divided in some groups.

When a family is composed of parents and married children, it is labelled as *extended family.*

(i) When such a family includes only married sons and their children it is known as *patrilineal extended family*, for example, Oraons, Mundas, Santals, Bengalis, etc.

(ii) When the extended family includes married daughters and their children it is known as *matrilineal extended family,* for example, Garo, Khasis, etc.

(iii) When an extended family is composed of many members or married couples of vertical and horizontal relation such a family is known as a *joint family.*

(iv) When a joint family is composed of the relatives belonging to fathers or male side only it is known as *patrilineal joint family,* for example, Bengalis.

(v) And if such a family includes relatives of mother side or female line only, it is known as *matrilineal joint family*, for example, Khasis and Nayars.

When a man marries more than one woman and all the wives live separately, then the family is a combination of couple of simple families with a common factor—father or husband.

Polygynous Family : Sometimes, all the wives live together with single husband, but their children are not distinguished to their mothers. The classic example is noticed among the Kulin Brahmins, Muslims, etc.

Polyandrous Family : As the name implies this form of family results from polyandrous system of marriage, i.e., when several men marry by one woman and live together. The Todas and the Tibetans enjoy this sort of family life.

'Deiri' types in Australia—a man belongs to two families simultaneously.

(1) with his original family, i.e., with a permanent wife, known as *Tippamalku.*

(2) with the temporary one, i.e., *Pirrauru.* It is known as composite family.

Among the Todas, polyandrous marriage is found, i.e., a group of men often marry one woman, side by side each man marrying individually. The polyandrous marriage here begets a polyandrous family along with simple family with it. So the combination of these two families result in a composite family among them.

Incomplete family: When a man marries a woman, but without children it is called the *Incomplete family*.

Broken family : Besides these, another form known as *loose or broken family* in which either of the parents dies without any remarriage, is also prevalent in all the human societies.

In Marquisan Islands, a number of unrelated persons join the household of a married woman of high status and participate jointly in her economic responsibilities and sexual privileges and they form together—a familiar unit labelled as a *Marquisan family*.

Therefore we may now say that the types of family mainly depend upon three conditions, i.e., social phenomena.

1. Rules of descent.
2. Residence after marriage.
3. Types of authority.

Feature

Common Residence

A residence is essential for each and every person as well as the family. A family consists of parents and children. Among the Hindus, it is a prevalent custom that the married couple should reside in the house of the parents. All the members of family share a common house for the protective measures against the environment and the external hostilities. It is also important to preserve his or her properties. There are chiefly two types of residences.

(i) patrilocal, e.g., Hindus, the English, etc.

(ii) matrilocal, e.g., Garo, Khasi, etc.

Division of Labour

Division of labour between man and woman is found in every society. The allocation of roles in a family follow a natural division of labour based on age and sex. The adjustment is almost universal to the families. The woman looks after the household work. She prepares food like the mother and repairs the clothing and gives all sorts of comfort to the man. Among the Eskimo society, this is a special feature for the male hunter. In the Hindu society, there is not only the division of labour but the wife remains faithful and loyal to her husband. In some societies, both men and women work together.

Reproduction

Another important feature is reproduction. By marriage, the individuals of opposite sexes come in closeness and biological relationship gets established. Offspring are born out of that biological union, forms groups with a bondage of blood relationship.

Kinship

By this method, the children are introduced to the relatives and they learn thereby to behave with the rest of the population according to the culture matrix.

Common Hearth or Kitchen

It is generally (but in rare cases) found in joint family especially among Bengalis.

Function

Functions of the families are so fundamental that almost in all societies, families are present and the families like a continuous network which encircle all the individuals living in the socictics. It is a condition where the human beings in an institutionalised way satisfy the basic unit to build normative behaviour in human relations.

Every social group has some special social function and status in the society where it exists. So the family has some functions to perform. It has of course manifold functions to discharge. They are —

I. (a) Physical cases of victimisation of its members, discharged through bodily harms and illness care of the victim or the invalid, or of the mother and child at birth.

(b) Provision and distribution of food, shelter and clothing.

(c) Provision for sex activity of the spouses and sometimes for other members as for the younger brothers in the Santal families. This is absent in the true consanguine family of the Nayars.

II. Transmission of culture pattern specially in childhood by training in eating, cleanliness, dress and decoration, speech and language, response to happiness, sorrows and miseries and finally behaviour and attitude towards others.

But from the anthropological point of view to study the human beings—both primitive and modern particularly with respect to the knowledge of the social conditions of the people in the field. The functions of the family are—

Economic function: It is divided into two groups.

(a) *Food Supply*: There is an arrangement among the people on the parts of both the husband and the wife to supply the food for subsistence. Men collect food by hunting, fishing or by agricultural means and the women collect roots, tubers, fruits, etc., whereas in agriculture, the women help men in the field and the preparation of food materials. In some societies, both men and women work together in their respective professions, i.e., in the factory, mine or tea garden, but the preparation of food and domestic duties are entrusted with other women folks.

(b) *Transmission of Property:* All the material resources of a person in a family or self-earned property of the parents must pass either through the sons or daughters as is observed in the patrilineal or the matrilineal family like the Santals or the Khasis. Thus the property remains within the group of kins.

Shelter

A shelter is necessary for each family for the protective against the environment and any external hostilities.

There are chiefly two types of residences—patrilocal and matrilocal—meaning residences in the father and mother's house respectively.

Patrilocal residence — The Hindus, the English.

Matrilocal residence — It is just the reverse of the former, e.g., Khasis, the Garos.

Caring and Rearing

In early infancy, the children are given tender care, food and shelter. In the atmosphere of family, the individuals are brought up and the infants require a long period of rearing, and they constantly require a persisting protection from social, environmental and economic evils. The mother looks after the child upto a certain age, then the father makes arrangement to give him or her education and teach the social traditions and customs.

Propagating the Tradition

Each and every family have some traditional cultural pattern. The family in all human societies functions to transmit the human culture through generation after generation. Transmission of such tradition of a family assumes importance in childhood by sustained training of every activities. Of course in some societies a part of such activities are done by formal associations like 'Ghotuls of the Muria and Abujmaria' 'Morung of the Nagas', etc.

Regulation of Sex Life

In family too, the sex life is regulated by the rule of family exogamy. It is the general rule that no member of the family will have sexual relationship with the persons who are related by blood from a common ancestor and hence no marriage is possible. The influence of family exogamy is extended to a longer duration, both on the father and the mother's family circles.

Family is a means of regular and channelised sexual gratification. Members of the family except husband and wife could not meet sexually.

Affiliation to Kins

The family serves as a unit to affiliate the relationship either through the father or the mother. The mothers come from another family group and her brother or sister is related to the children of the family through the mother as maternal uncle or aunt (*mama* or *mausi*), similarly the father's brother or sister as paternal uncle or aunt (*kaka* or *jeta,* or *pisi*) either younger or elder brother to father and sister is related.

So the use of family names where it occurs are known by the children of a family after he or she introduces to the relatives and thereby they learn to behave with the rest of the population according to the cultural matrix.

Marriage

Marriage is the socially sanctioned union of male and female who are thereby entitled to enjoy the sexual right and the right to reproduce legitimate offspring. In the language of Westermark "it is a relation of one or more men to one or more women which is recognised by custom or law and involves certain rights and duties, both in the case of the parties entering the union and in the case of the children born of it". The right of sexual intercourse is always implied in marriage. The society gives allowance to such intercourse in the case of the husband and the wife. Besides the regulated sexual relations marriage has other factors. It is an institution. The husband should maintain his wife and children. Moreover, there are other social and ceremonial aspects of marriage. The performance of the union is to be done according to the rules laid down by customs or law. The consent of the parties and their parents are also required.

Regarding the forms of marriage the anthropologists are not univocal. 'Lowie' in his 'Social Organisation' dealt the outlawed, reprobated, accepted or approved forms of mating as forms of marriage. To him those are "levirate, fillial widow inheritance, the sororate, union with the daughter of the wife's sister, with the sisters' daughter, and symmetrical cross-cousin marriage". But one should remember that in cultural anthropology few words like "laws of marriage" to explain the exogamy and endogamy, etc., preferential mating to explain the levirate, sororate, cross-cousin marriage and parallel cousin marriage are also used. So the question arises, if everything can be included within the concept of 'form' why other words or terminologies have arose. And how shall one entitle the concepts about polygamy, group marriage, etc. Etymologically a 'form' means 'shape', 'order', or 'system', and a type means—'a species', 'a kind'. However, for the sake of convenience—the type and form are held as synonymous and are entitled to denote the following forms of marriage.

Monogamy: It means single marriage, that is, marriage of a man with a woman. It is widely prevalent among the Australians, Bushman, Santal, Dhodia, Veddas (scheduled tribes), Negritos of Philippine. African Pygmies and also among the industrially advance section of the world population. Monogamy gives all the members of the society to enjoy life equally and thereby, helps to maintain social balance and due to such practice, it is considered as the common form of marriage.

Polygamy: It means plural marriage. It has two sub-forms.

(a) *Polygyny* : The marriage of a single man simultaneously to a number of women, who are contemporary to one another. In India it prevails everywhere. It was very common and prestigious social norm among the Kulin Brahmins of Bengal. Beside various tribal groups of Indian subcontinent like Kuki, Naga, Siddi, Ho, Gond, etc., does allow the practice of multiple wives. Among the Muslims, this is very common feature. Africa is held as the paradise or home of polygyny.

(b) *Polyandry:* The marriage of a woman simultaneously to a number of men, who are contemporary to one another. Polyandry is much restricted in distribution. In tribal pockets of India, it is found among the Todas of Nilgiri Hills, the Khasas of Juansar Bawar, the Ladakhi Bhotia, etc. It is reported that the Todas of Nilgiri practise such a social custom owing to their strong belief in the direct descendency from the Royal family of the Pandavas. Rivers pointed out the practise of *female infanticide* to be responsible for the introduction of polyandry among the Todas. The Ladakhi brothers marry only one woman just to avoid the division of their ancestral property like houses and agricultural lands. S.C. Roy reported that in central Tibet, a father enlists his name as a marital partner of his son's wife and similarly sons may exercise marital rights over the second wife of their father. It is held that in historic India polyandry was a prevalent form of marriage among the people living in the region extending from Kashmir to Assam. Radcliffe Brown points out that *adelphic* or *fraternal* form of polyandry is due to what, he terms, the unity and solidarity of the sibling group.

Polyandry is of two types:

(i) *Fraternal* or *adelphic* —Where the husbands of a woman are related as brothers—commonly found in Tibet, Todas of Nilgiri.

(ii) *Non-fraternal* —Where the husbands are not related as brothers; found among Khasas of

Juansar Bawar. The Nayars of South India have non-fraternal polyandry.

Early evolutionists like McLenan and Morgan considered polyandry as a stage in the evolution of marriage. Westermarck postulated the following causes for the introduction of polyandry in different societies like ill-proportion in numerical strength of the population structure due to female infanticide, poverty, high demand of bride price, overall backwardness. Control over property for which the encouragement of joint family system and lastly it also acts as a device for population control. Lowie also advocated that existence of polyandry among the Todas and the Eskimos is due to ill proportion in numerical strength of the population.

Group Marriage

The Eskimos lend their wives for shorter or longer periods and establish strong friendship. These extra-marital relations have erroneously been called group-marriage. McLenan and Herbert Muller say that sexual communism prevails in the early stage of society and group marriage is only one step higher from the promiscuous condition. White remarked that in Tibet, Bhutan and Sikkim, three brothers can marry sisters and all the wives remain with them.

Marriage Rules

In the regulation of marriage, notion of kinship and determination of the range of prohibited degree are two important factors. Kinship prohibition sometimes taken into consideration for disallowing a marital alliance.

In settling a marriage the lineage is considered primarily. Lineage exogamy which regulates marriage among all the tribes excepting some endogamous ones. The tribes having no clan, organisation, lineage and kinship are considered. But those having clan, system, operation of lineage exogamy remain unimportant. Among the tribes namely, Maler, Saora, Mahadev Koli, Dubla, Kadar, and Andamanese who do not possess any clan system, lineage exogamy and kinship notion regulate such marriages. Radcliffe Brown (1948) writes that the only regulation of marriage among the Andamanese, is the kinship. Marriage is forbidden between the near consanguines. Besides the rules like tribal endogamy, phratry exogamy, moiety exogamy and clan exogamy are observed by the majority of the Indian tribes. There are other rules like, clan agamy and clan endogamy. Clan agamy permitting marriage within and outside a clan is observed from a number of tribes, such as, Lakher, Chero, Kharia, Riang and Jaunsari, while clan endogamy is the rule in the regulation of marriage among Hill Miri, Lushai and Kol. There are three other rules to regulate marriage, which are prevalent in the Map of Tribal India.

(a) *Village* or *Local Exogamy.* It was the result of localisation of an agnatic group of exogamous lineage or a clan in a village or in an area. The inherent concept that overrules any possibility of marriage within a village was the kinship notion of consanguinity. Village exogamy is practised by Aka, Gallong, Chero, Bhil, Bondo, etc.

(b) *Regional Endogamy.* It is another unstructured principle of marriage regulation observed by Dubla (Shah, 1958) and Bhil (Naik, 1956). Shah remarked that the principle of *gotra* is not observed rigidly by the Dubla while the concept of *vito* (circle) is important for regulation of marriage. The bride is usually selected within *vito.*

(c) *Ceremonial Kinship.* The ceremonial or putative kinship sometimes function as a regulation of marital alliance among some tribes like Ao Naga, Bondo, Chero, Oraon who regard this as sacred. Among the Ao Naga, this relationship is locally known as *Atombu* (Mill, 1926) and among Bondo it is known as *moitur* (Elwin, 1950), among Oraon and Chero it is known as *sahaiya* or *phooldair*.

Exogamy: Exogamy indicates the rule that a man must marry someone outside his own group. The limits may be family lineage, clan, phratry, moiety, etc.

Endogamy: It refers to the rule that a man must marry someone within his own social group. Such as the Hindu castes are endogamous entities, different tibal groups are also endogamous in nature. The Shiya and Sunni sect of Muslim community are also endogamous.

Hypergamy: When a man gets his daughter married to a person of the higher social and economic status. This type of alliance was called as *anuloma.* The Kulin Brahman and Kayasthas of Bengal had such a system in the recent past.

Hypogamy: When a daughter is married with a man of lower social and economic status, this alliance was called as *pratiloma.* It is reported that Brahman girls married to Sudra man and their offspring became known as *Chandal*—the untouchable.

Mode of Acquiring Mates

The way by which a tribe acquire his life partner are of various in nature, which are described in the following lines. Religious rites and rituals are not absolute things in their marriage alliances.

(i) *Negotiation Marriage:* When the parents of both

the boy and girl settle the marital alliance for their children marriage.

(ii) *Marriage by Purchase:* It is one of the prevalent way of acquiring mate in tribal societies of India, like Santal, Munda, Oraon, Gond, etc., and where the payment of bride-price system exist, that is, payment made to the family of bride.

(iii) *Marriage by Service:* To acquire a wife by rendering service to his (bridegroom) prospecting father-in-law's house and in agricultural field. The system is widespread in the tribal pockets of India. It may be taken as an alternative measure of marriage by bride price. This system is prevalent in various tribal groups of Chotanagpur, Muria, and Maria Gonds of Bastar, Korku of Melaghat, Baiga of Madhya Pradesh, Purum and Chiru Kukis of Manipur, etc.

(iv) *Marriage by Capture:* The practise of smearing vermilion on the parting line of hairs on the forehead of the girl at a market place or any important place by the boy and fully surprise the girl and when the boy fleds away from the place. If the boy manages to run away safely from the spot before the arrival of the kinsmen of the girl, the social marriage will be held without payment of bride price. This type of marriage is found among Hos, Oraon, Birhor of Chotanagpur region.

(v) *Marriage by Elopement:* Among the Birhor, Ho and Santal tribes, the boy and the girl leave their parental houses in hide and with both of their mutual consent get married outside. After spending long time outside or after having a child, the couple returns to the village when their marital alliance is socially accepted after offering a community feast to the village elders.

(vi) *Marriage by Intrusion:* This type of marriage occurs among the Santal, Birhor and Hos of Singhbhum area. If a girl desires to marry an unwilling boy, she applies force to get his consent. She waits for a suitable opportunity and on getting such advantage she enters the boy's house without seeking any permission from the house members and engage herself in domestic chores. If she tolerates abusing, and other ill-treatments met by the mother and sisters of the boy for a specific time period, then she will given recognition of a wife of the boy and the usual marriage function will be organised later on.

(vii) *Remarriage:*In tribal societies, both the bridegroom and bride have their equal rights for divorce and remarriage. After divorce, the marriage can be held again without payment of bride price.

(viii) *Marriage by inheritance:* Inheritance of widow is one of the important ways of acquiring mate as found among some tribal groups.

Preferential Marriage

Levi-strauss remarked that the main aim of such alliance is to strengthen the in-group feeling among the tribe, while Tylor and Lowie stated that such marriages help in keeping the property among the close kin group. The preferential matings are of four categories.

(i) *Parallel Cousin Marriage:* The marriage between the children of either two brothers or two sisters, is practiced among the Muslim community.

(ii) *Cross-Cousin Marriage:* When marriages are held among the children of uterine brother and sister. It is found among the Toto, Abujmaria, Bison-Horn Maria, Muria, Bhatra, etc.

(iii) *Levirate:* It is the marriage between a widow with her deceased husband's younger brother. This is also prevalent in various tribal groups of India.

(iv) *Sororate:* A widower marries with his deceased wife's sister especially younger one. It is found almost in all the societies.

Kinship

Kinship is the cementing factor in between family and marriage. In the human society, people are found together in groups by various kinds of bonds. These bonds are chiefly based on reproduction. The first kind of such bond is affinal-kin means the bond between spouses and their relatives on either side while the second kind of bond or relationship based on blood ties, called consanguineal-kin, that is, bond between parents and their children and that between siblings.

A kinship system, however, is not a social group nor does it correspond ever to an organised aggregation of individuals. It is merely, as the name implies, a structural system of relationship in which individuals are bound and one to another by complex interlocking and ramifying ties, particular kinship bonds isolated from others may and often do serve to unite individuals into social groups, such as a nuclear family or a lineage, but kinship system as wholes are not and do not produce social aggregates. The point of departure for the analysis of kinship is the nuclear family.

To understand the social structure of a society through kinship behaviours of the people within the family and its outer world is important. An adult individual in a society usually belongs to two nuclear families viz., (a) family of orientation and (b) family of procreation and ramifying series of such links which bind members or individuals to one another through kinship ties. The role and status of such individual vary according to the situation which gives rise to kinship system. With the help of kinship system, the social structure of a tribe or a community can be understood. Broadly, the kinship system can be analysed in the following way.

Radcliffe Brown has pointed out that specially the range of application of the kinship terms and the specific behaviours of the persons give the full account of the dynamic relationship within a society.

Structure of kinship roles may further be divided into two parts: (A) types of relationship, (B) kinship terms.

(A) types of relationship are primarily of two kinds :

(1) Real, i.e., actual.

(2) Virtual or artificial, i.e., ceremonial kins, social kins, etc.

(1) Real kins are of two kinds—

(a) Consanguinal—those of blood relations.

(b) Affinal—those after marriage relations.

The term primary relative is applied to those who belong to the same nuclear family as a particular person. In nuclear families only father, mother, sisters, brothers in the family of orientation and husband or wife, his sons and daughters in the family of procreation. In extended family or joint family or in polygynous or polyandrous or composite families (Toda), the primary relatives are more in number.

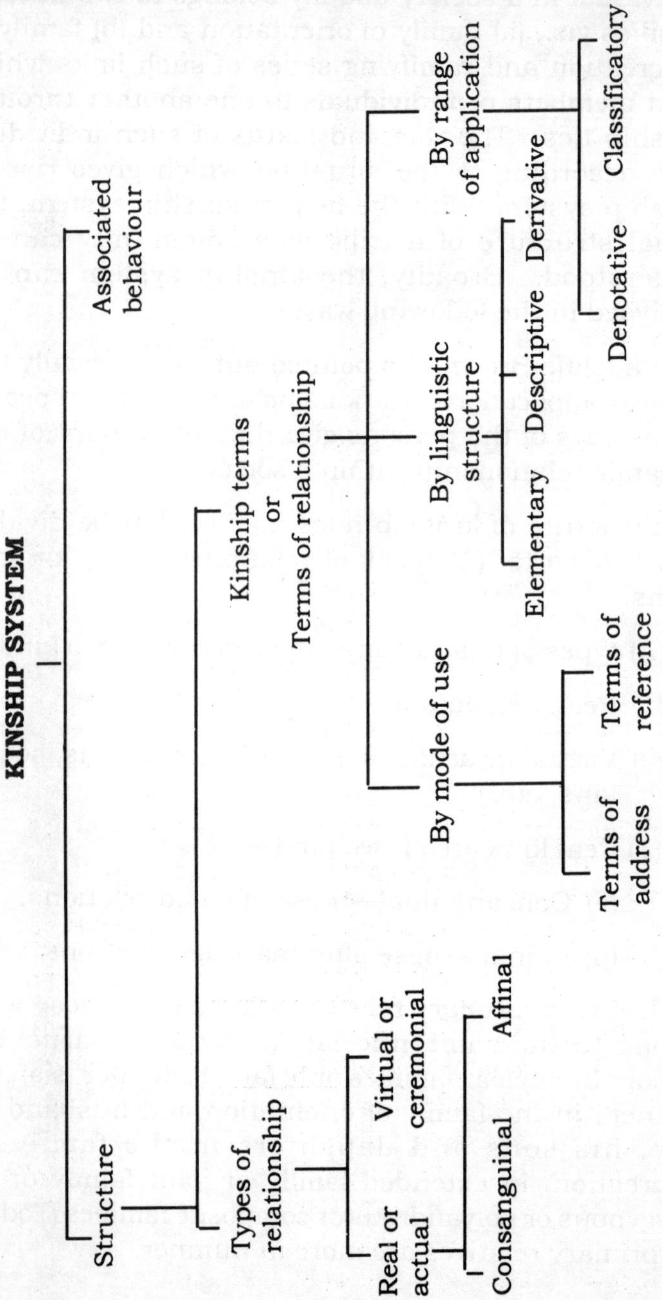
KINSHIP SYSTEM
Structure
Associated behaviour
Types of relationship
Kinship terms or Terms of relationship
Real or actual
Virtual or ceremonial
Consanguinal
Affinal
By mode of use
By linguistic structure
By range of application
Terms of address
Terms of reference
Elementary
Descriptive
Derivative
Denotative
Classificatory

Secondary relatives are primary relatives of each primary relatives of ego. Each secondary relative has primary relatives who are tertiary relatives. More remote than tertiary relatives are distant relatives.

The relatives between whom every connecting relationship is one of blood or common ancestry are actually-consanguinal relatives or kins. When the bond between two relatives—primary or secondary or tertiary or remote is based on marital ties are classed as affinal relatives or kins. Relatives are classed by some other terms as : agnate those related through father or masculine only. *Cognate* those related through mother or father line or both; *uterine* relatives of mothers side only. An interesting common usage intermediate between the personal names and kinship terms is called *teknonymy.* In its typical form, it consists in calling a person who has had a child—"father or so and so" , combining the parental term with the child's name instead of using a personal name or a kinship term. (*Ogo* or *Khokarma* in Bengali).

(B) Kinship terms are technically classified in three different ways—(i) By their mode of use: a term of 'address' is the one used in speaking to a relative, it is a part of the linguistic behaviour, characteristic of the particular interpersonal relationship. A term of 'reference' is the one used to designate a relative in speaking about him to a third person expressing particular kinship status. The term of 'relation' is sometime same with term of address or term of reference or different terms of reference are usually more complete than terms of address. (ii) By the linguistics structure —the kinship terms are distinguished as 'elementary' or irreducible word (Baba or father, Ma), which cannot be analysed into component lexical elements with kinship meanings. A 'derivative' term is one (which like grandfather or *Meso Mosay* in Bengali), which is compounded from an elementary term of some lexical element that does not have primarily a kinship meaning. A 'descriptive' term is one which (*Masi-Ma* in Bengali)—combines two more elementary terms to denote a specific relative. (iii) As regards the range of application, kinship terms are differentiated as : 'Denotative'—applies only to relative in a single kinship category as defined by generation, sex and genealogical connection. 'Classificatory'—applies to persons of two or more kinship categories as defined by generation, sex and genealogical connection. Study or implication of the classificatory terms is important as this has intricate relation with the kinship behaviour in particular societies. There are six major criteria, when linguistically recognised as a basis of terminological differentiation will yield denotative terms but ignoring any one of which produces classificatory terms. The criteria are generation, sex, affinity, collaterality, bifurcation and polarity. The above structure had to be understood against the associated behaviour at the following levels :

(a) Interpersonal relationship between kins within the household.

(b) Interpersonal relationship outside the household (among the consanguinal kins).

(c) Interpersonal relationship outside the household among the affinals and ceremonial or village kins.

(d) Behaviour of the kins both consanguinal and affinal at different rites of passage from birth to death.

(e) Behaviour of kins in secular affairs, i.e., economic or in factional affairs.

The above theme may be observed after illustrations. I. Karve has rightly said that three things are absolutely necessary for the understanding of any cultural phenomenon in India. These are : configuration of linguistic regions, the institution of caste and the family organisation (Karve, 1968). Here as per scope only family organisation is discussed :

Family system among the following communities are as follows—

(a) *Hindu chasi* (peasant). Among these people, the family includes parents and married sons, normally with brothers, their married sons and older parents, widowed sisters or father's sisters (three generations).

(b) *Gandhabaniks* (merchant). Among them, big families including married brothers (own or cousin) with their married sons, old parents and their brothers (three generations) are more commonly found.

(c) *Muslim peasants*. Among them, the parents and married sons are common, sometimes married brothers with their married sons and old parents are also found (three generations). A notable feature in some cases is a man marries more than one woman and all the wives and their children live together with the husband. Sometimes, the marriage between son and daughter of two brothers is also found.

(d) *Santals* : Among these agricultural tribe—family is normally composed of parents and sometimes one or two married sons also live with the old parents. "The widest separate unit is the 'clan', the kinship groups within the clan are the subclan, the local lineage of the extended family, all of which are patrilineal ... . The local lineage is a group of patrilineal male—kins men living within a few miles of one another, periodically worshipping as a unit, and gathering together on such occasions as marriages and funerals. It is the largest corporate group within the kinship system. The patrilineal, patrilocal extended family is a distinctive economic and ritual. Social unit which often occupies a single house site, though common residence and economic unity seldom are maintained after the death of the father of the family or the marriage of all of his sons. The nuclear families which together composed the extended family are distinguishable units and provide the line of fracture by which the extended family divides itself. All interaction among Santals is in part regulated by kinship. For a traditional Santal, it is really impossible to establish a relationship of any depth except on the firm bedrock of kinship" (Orans, 1965).

(e) *Khasis of Khasi Hills—Meghalaya* : Among these horticultural tribes, the family is composed of parents and with one or two married daughters—compulsorily including the married youngest daughter and old parents.

(f) *Todas of Nilgiri Hills, South India* : Among these pastoral tribes, the family is composed of husbands (who are brothers) with wife and children.

It is found that generally each family structure mentioned above includes certain kins. Each structure is composed of certain roles. In each case kinship, tie is the fundamental principle for the given structure. It is the cementing factor for the formation of the respective family grouping. Each role performs certain functions, i.e., economic, reproductive, child rearing, religious and educative. Rights and duties are reciprocally performed. The (a),(d),(e) type families, i.e., with married sons/daughters, the parents are labelled as extended. In (b) type family, the family includes more such relatives—known as joint family. The (c) type family with more than one wife and children sharing meal from same hearth are labelled as polygynous family, where the children cannot be identified according to their mothers. The (f) type family is labelled as polyandrous family. These types are approached more closely and analytically, during studies.

Economy as favoured by ecology at the very basic level in each case controls the size of the structure. In the (b) type, market is the chief factor controlling the structure. In the (c) type family, immediately the marriage and ultimately the religion, these two factors are responsible for the size and structure. The number of wives and marriage between parallel brothers and sisters, i.e., children of the two brothers are favoured by the religion. However, the type of marriage is entirely responsible for the structure of (f) type family.

Law of descent and religion are responsible for the (e) type family structure. Thus economy, religion and law of descent—these three factors are responsible for the structure of the above family types. These factors have an impact on the family function, which is chiefly related to child rearing process and education in the respective type, which exerts the impact on the process of socialisation or formation of personality in the respective communities.

Generally, four basic factors are responsible for the formation of family grouping. These are:

(a) Sex urge;

(b) Sex division of labour;

(c) Common shelter or residence and

(d) Care and conditioning of the children.

In India, particularly among the Hindus, family is the basic unit for four stages or 'Ashramas' of human life, which is meant for performing the worldly and other worldly activities (*chaturashrama*). This is the primary set up of *ashramas* for performing *kartavyas* (duties) and *kriya-karmas* in this world which is directly linked with the other worlds, where these will be reflected and results bestowed in this life and at the next birth accordingly. So *Griha* or residence is the seat for the family, where wife is not only a bed-mate or economic partner, she is the *Dharma Sangini* —for *Patni* means she rescues the husband from the *pat naraka* (a type of hell). If a man living in the *Sansar* remain unmarried will be subjected to that *Naraka.* She also adorns the house—as *grihini griha muchyate.* Again *putrarthe kriyate barya* means—wife is essential for having the son. As son or *putra* rescues the parents from *punnam naraka* (a type of hell). All these are the themes for *Dharmanusthana* which are cultural. So, the family among the Hindus is not a grouping merely for satisfaction of material and biological needs, but aimed at certain meaningful cultural attainments which is intimately and inseparably related to the entire Hindu philosophy. Here the Hindu family organisation differs totally from the family organisations in the west. The mode of teaching of the traditional norms and values in the family for forming Hindu personality always help (helped?) to nourish the cultural or human elements over the biological instincts and sheer material necessities. Marriage rules, and values also convey the same principles, where the kinship structure and functions are attuned accordingly.

This type or method of study is known as structural functional analysis. It shows the interdependence of the family, marriage and kinship studies on the one hand and discloses any similaritics and differences in the basic social or cultural behaviour structure affecting the personality formation among different Indian communities on the other. For studying the Hindu family—marriage and kinship analysis from cultural point of view would be helpful, where interactions are observed on the basis of *Sastriya* and *laukik acharas.* That shows clearly the relation between the regional part cultures with the total or whole Hindu tradition. If such an understanding is further extended at the levels of social stratification, then the social change gives us a total picture of any community—primitive or contemporary at a particular time and space.

Murdock, following the lead offered by Leslie Spier tries to simplify the complexities of kinship terminologies of the world. His classification, however, rests around cousins. Murdock's major systems of kinship terminology are—Eskimo, Hawaian, Iroquois,Sudanese, Omaha and Crow system.

(i) *Eskimo.* Fa Si Da and Mo Br Da are called by the same terms as parallel cousins, but terminologically differentiated from sisters; the term for the two cross-cousins are usually but not always the same. Children of Fa Si and children of Mo Br and children of Fa Br have the same terms, but different what they use for their own brother and sister. Example—Andamanese of Andaman Islands, Dimasa—Kachari of Assam.

(ii) *Hawaian.* All cross and parallel cousins called by the same terms as those used for sisters and brothers. Example—Lakher (Mizoram), Purum (Manipur), Riang (Tripura), Bhumij, Ho, Oroan,

Santal, Chero (Bihar), Bondo (Orissa) and Kol (Madhya Pradesh).

(iii) *Iroquois.* Fa Si Da and Mo Br Da called by the same terms but terminologically differentiated from parallel cousins as well as from sisters; parallel cousins commonly but not always classified with sisters, that is, children of Fa Si and Mo Br have same terms which are different from what is used towards parallel cousins as well as their own siblings. Example—Rabha (West Bengal), Birjia (Bihar), Bhumia, Kamar, Maria Gond, Baiga (Madhya Pradesh), Chenchu, Hill Reddi (Andhra Pradesh), Garo, Khasi, Pnar (Meghalaya), etc.

(iv) *Sudanese.* This is a system of kin terminology in which each cousin is called by a separate term.

(v) *Omaha.* Fa Si Da and Mo Br Da called by different terms and terminologically differentiated from sisters and parallel cousins, but Fa Si Da is terminologically classed with Si Da and or Mo Br Da with Mo Si. Example—Lushai (Mizoram), Thado Kuki (Manipur), Ao Naga, Sema Naga, Angami Naga, Rengama Naga (Nagaland).

(vi) *Crow.* Fa Si Da and Mo Br Da, are called by different terms and terminologically differentiated from sisters and parallel cousin, but father's sister's daughter is terminologically classed with Si Da and Mo Br Da with Mo Si.

It was Spier (1925) and Lowie (1929), who first attempted typological classification of kinship terms. The basis of Spier's classification was the term for female cross-cousins applied by males and that of Lowie was the treatment of collateral as compared with the lineal kin in the first ascending and descending generation.

Features of Lowie's four system

System	*Identity of Terms*
(i) Generation	Fa = Fa Br = Mo Br
(ii) Bifurcate Merging	Fa = Fa Br; Mo Br (e.g. Tangas (Arunachal), Lakher, Lushai (Mizoram), Baiga (M.P.), Chenchu, Hill Reddy (A.P.), Thado Kuki (Manipur), Angami Naga, Ao Naga, Sema Naga (Nagaland), Garo, Pnar (Meghalaya), Oraon, Santal (Bihar), Kota, Toda (Tamil Nadu), Kadar, Urali (Kerala).
(iii) Bifurcate Collateral	Fa; Fa Br; Mo Br (e.g. Adi, Idu Mishmi (Arunachal), Rabha (West Bengal), Mikir (Assam), Asur, Birhor, Chero, Ho, Maler, Bhumij, Birja (Bihar), Bondo, Juang, Kharia (Orissa), Tharu (U.P.), Kamar, Maria Gond, Kol, (M.P.), Bhil (Gujarat).
(iv) Lineal	Fa; Fa Br = Mo Br e.g. Riang (Tripura).

Recent Development of Kinship Studies

In the modern period, there have been a number of new directions in the study of kinship which involve both method and theory. Some of these include cross cultural comparisons involving statistical and correlational techniques, others involve linguistics analysis building on Kroeber's earlier categories or utilising formal analysis, still others utilise models of various types, some derived from linguistics and others from mathematics. These studies have stimulated a great amount of new research and promise to broaden our knowledge of kinship phenomena in various directions.

Of particular significance is Murdock's cross cultural study of family and kinship organisation in about 250 societies throughout the world, presented in social structure (1949). Utilising the postulational method and statistical analysis he found that kinship terminologists are primarily determined by such sociological factors as descent and residence, with marriage rules of lesser importance. He then established six types of kinship terminology, bored in part on Spier's earlier classification and combined these with the rules of descent and residence to give eleven major types of social organisation. A proposed order of social change beginning with the changes in residence pattern was then tested against the evidence from linguistic reconstructions and other data was found highly reliable. "It seems clear", Murdock wrote "that the elements of social organisation, in their permutations and combinations, conform to natural laws of their own with an exactitude scarcely less striking than that which characterises the permutations and combinations of atoms in chemistry or genes in biology" (1949, p.163).

Murdock's study represents a notable advance in the application of social science methodologies to the study of social organisation, but there has been considerable criticism of sampling involved, the statistical techniques used and the data selected for analysis—responded with the more adequate *World Ethnographic Sample* (1957) and with a revised classification (1959, pp. 135-40) of five major types of social organisations based primarily on descent and residence patterns. He has also modified the assumptions about the primary role of residence in bringing about the social changes.

The contribution of Levi-Strauss to the study of kinship systems are of a different character, and in *Les structures eleminataires de la parente* (1949) and *Structural Anthropology* (1958), he presents some highly original views on the nature of social structure in general kinship in particular. *Social Structure*, for Levi-Strauss, is in itself concerned not with the empirical reality of social relations, but with models which gives rise to them, and he discusses the relevance of mechanical models (those on the same scale as the phenomena) and statistical models (where the elements of the models are on different scale) for various problems, particularly those of communication. With regard to kinship, he views the terminology and the system of attitudes as representing quite different orders of reality. "The modalities of behaviour between relatives express to some extent the terminological classification, and they provide at the same time a means of overcoming difficulties and contradictions resulting from this classification" (1958, 1963) a dialectic which is responsible for change in both systems. Levi-Strauss also proposes some different units for kinship studies from the elementary family, which is favoured by Malinowski, Radcliffe Brown, Murdock and others. He believes "the relationship between brothers-in-law is the axis around which kinship structure is built" (1958, 1963) and thus adds the wife's brother to the family unit. All kinship structures are constructed on this "kinship atom", primarily by the organisation of a series of oppositions between attitudes of familiarity and reserve. The resulting kinship system "does not consist in the objective ties of descent or consanguinity between individuals. It exists only in human consciousness; it is an arbitary system of representations, not spontaneous development of real situation". (*ibid*)

The principal reciprocity, as manifested in various forms of exchange in social life, is central to Levi-Strauss's view of social instructions. Kinship in human society is established and perpetuated through specified forms of marriage as a form of exchange that involves with the circulation of women. He is therefore, particularly concerned with what he calls "elementary structures" or those characterised by preferential marriage with a particular category of kin, usually a "cross-cousin". In this respect, Levi-Strauss has attempted the analysis of matrilateral cross-cousin marriage systems, which are found in Australia, South Eastern and Eastern Asia as well as in a few other regions, where the resulting dual structure was of "wife-giving" and "wife-receiving" groups reflected in many aspects of society and culture.

This complex and original contribution (summarised in English in de Josselin de Young 1952) has stimulated a number of important studies and engendered considerable controversy. Homans and Sohneider, in *Marriage, Authority, and Final Causes* (1955) essay-an alternate explanation based on Radcliffe—Brown's theory of sentiments. Needham attacked this strongly in *Structure and Sentiment* (1962) and went on to make a number of reformulation of what he calls "prescriptive" marriage systems. Leach in *Rethinking Anthropology* (1961), shows the considerable influence of *Levi-Strauss*, as does Cumont, whose *Hierarchy and Marriage Alliance in South Indian Kinship* (1957) emphasises the importance of treating certain categories of relatives as affinal rather to consanguinal.

In recent years, a number of anthropologists and

linguists have returned to Kroeber's analysis (1909) of kinship terminologies and have developed a more sophisticated approach, called *componential analysis*. The general framework for componential analysis derives from linguistic theory, and kinship vocabulary is regarded as constituting a paradigm which can be analysed in the same manner as other paradigmatic sets in a language. Currently, Lounsbury et al. are attempting to contrast the theories using a limited number of ordered roles similar to those of "generative grammar". The resulting "formal account" specifies (1) a set of primitive elements and (2) a set of rules for operating on these to generate a model, which represents the empirical data (Lounsbury, 1964).

Goodenough (1956) treats Kroeber's categories as essentially the social components, but Lounsbury (1956) and Buchler's (1964) analyses are based upon strict genealogical reckoning and operate in terms of the primary relations amongst the nuclear family and their extensions to more distant relatives. Lounsburry assumes that "the primary function of kinship terminologies is to delineate the relation of ego to the members of the personal kindred in such a way as to express some socially and legally important aspect of each of these relationships" (1964, p. 382). Friedrich in *Semantic Structure and Social Structure : An Instance from Russian*, is concerned with noticing their interrelationships—"The Semantic network symbolises and is generated by the social networks is significant, because it can lead to yet more general inferences about native concepts" (1964, p. 132). And H.C.Conklin, in *Ethnogenealogical Method*, illustrates the steps which may be taken from ethnographic description to final analysis.

The sequence we have followed has led us from specific to general and abstract to correlational substatements of Hununoo ethnography. We have moved from individuals occupying the established genealogical positions in a well recognised kin net, to the examination of types of kin classes, to the analysis and articulation of the defining features are significant, which underlie the whole category system and finally to a brief consideration of one set of significant non-terminological correlates of the more highly structured parts of this system. In this procedure, he finds that the natives "model" of their own system is an important part of the data.

The utilisation of mathematical models for the elucidation of kinship structures have had a long history, beginning with John Dalton (1889) and continuing with Weil's appendix (1949) to Levi-Strauss's monograph and, most recently, H.C. Whites application of matrix algebra (1963). White is particularly concerned with the prescriptive marriage systems, such as the Kariera, Arunta, Murngin, and Purum, but is remains to be demonstrated whether logical manipulation of kinship categories and marriage rules adds greatly to our understanding of kinship system.

What do people perceive, think and know? How do people perceive think and know? These questions are of interest to both anthropology and psychology, but psychology concerns with second question while anthropology is primarily concerned with former one. Language is a fundamental aspect of culture. It occupies a position in cognitive studies and as the development of the study of psycho-linguistics. Language is employed in many cognitive processes.

In the terminology of semantics, a linguistic expression designates a class of image or concepts. To say that the 'sky is full of thunder cloud', is to designate a class or type of weather condition. Componential analysis is concerned solely with the significant aspect of meaning, componential analysis has been directed primarily at systematically contrasting the sets of denotation of the several expressions within single domains or sub domains.

3 Society, Culture and Civilisation

It is our primary duty to know our society, without this basic understanding we cannot claim our heritage. It is a fact that without such understanding how a relationship between our country and our men can start and grow? Without proper relation based on clear understanding how can there grow true will for the welfare of our society. In anthropology, especially in its branch, social-cultural anthropology has a very fruitful method of understanding the society, that is, all types of social-cultural relationship and social interactions in any community—primitive or contemporary. It is a fact that though each discipline of the social sciences has its own field and distinct methods of tackling its problems, still, findings of any discipline in social sciences are not independent, they are inter-related in such a manner that the propositions of one cannot be understood properly without the help of others.

Social-cultural anthropology may be described in the following ways, it studies human social and cultural process comparatively. Social process means the operation of the social life, the manner in which the actions and very existence of each living being affected those of other individuals with which it has relations.

The problem with which the social-cultural anthropologist is concerned when framed in a very general way, are of such order as—what are the main patterns of human behaviour in any society (primitive or contemporary) ? How far does conformity to these patterned relationships draw people together in groups? How do the groups interact to allow of the operation of what can be called a society? What are the controls for group action and for individual action of an interpersonal kind? How far do rational considerations enter in the field of controls? What are the sets of norms and value which give meaning to the behaviour of people in social circumstances? By what symbols do they express values? How do the patterns of behaviour stand up to changed circumstances? What kind of authority and guidance does tradition supply? How can values and symbols change? What kind of strain are most severe on human relationship? Thus, social-cultural anthropology by nature studies all sorts of human relations and behaviours, patterns of interaction of all societies and cultures. The distinguishing feature of social-cultural anthropology is the intensive detailed character of the systematic observation of the behaviour of people in group relation. Its enquiry is holistic in implication and it is comparative (Firth, 1951). The social-cultural anthropologist understands the society as any group of people who have lived and worked together long enough to get themselves organised to think of themselves as a social unit with well-defined limits. By culture he understands—historically created designs for living explicit and implicit, rational, irrational and non-rational, which exist at any given time as potential guides for the behaviour of man.

Thus, "if society is taken to be an aggregate of people and relations between them; culture emphasises the component of accumulated resources, immaterial as well as material which the people inherit, employ, transmute add to end transmit" (Firth, 1951). In 1920's social-cultural anthropologists studied only simpler or primitive societies. But by the late 1950's anthropologists were studying in small towns and cities, still using their technique of participant observation and interviewing... in the 1960's ... the study of process such as the cultural emulation of higher groups by lower groups, the maintenance of the local hierarchy of status and power, the incorporation of western scientific thoughts into indigenous thought and the past and present effects of indigenous political systems on modern politics have become the goal. Increasingly, anthropologists have been concerned not only with the analytical processes but also with the cultural models (Cohn, 1971).

Social-cultural anthropology studies society as a whole both primitive and contemporary. In technique, it depends mainly on personal observation, supplemented by records of case histories. The observer here attempts to understand and experience the norms and patterns of behaviour of people under study by staying among them. Thus he studies human behaviour by contextualisation. Here the object of study and observer belong to the same category; this facilitates him to understand directly his subject for which he is permitted by similar experiences and feelings. For this, some difficulties also arise as the behaviours vary from society to society, so it is hardly possible to find out similar units for common use everywhere. To overcome this difficulty systematic comparison is done here. Taken as a whole social-cultural anthropology is related to natural sciences in a generalised way, i.e., in sharing the comparative method and method of classification, though not in object of study. It is essentially a discipline of the social sciences sometimes approaching the field of humanities. It is often difficult to erect rigid boundaries among the disciplines of social sciences. As mentioned before, each has its own techniques of approach, but they are interrelated in such a manner that the propositions of one cannot be understood properly without help of the others. Observations and explanations of social-cultural anthropology are immediately benefited by the findings of sociology, history, psychology, political science and economics.

Now we are to know how the social-cultural anthropology approaches the societies analytically for an understanding. The object of our study is the social-cultural behaviours, accordingly tools adopted here are also of conceptual level. All social behaviours are primarily classified by their nature into two classes: (a) groupings and (b) institutions.

According to Nadel, a group may be defined as a collection of individuals who stand in regular and relatively permanent relationships, i.e., who act towards and in respect of each other, or towards and in respect of individuals outside the group and regularly in a specific and expectable and expected fashion ..... A group is composed of persons and the persons always defined in terms of modes of action in respect of others has its locus in the group. A person may belong to different groups and different persons may belong in one group. Such as—(1) Kin groups (2) Household (3) Lineage (4) Clan (5) Moiety (6) Tribe (7) Community : the maximal group of persons who normally reside together in face to face—association. The community and nuclear family are only universal social groupings. Communities differ in type with their mode of life as Bands (Primitive)—local groups .... The community may assume the form of a village or of a neighbourhood (Murdock, 1949). A community may form basing on factors like religion or language or occupational pattern.

According to Nadel by institution mean a standardised mode of social behaviour or since social behaviour means—co-activity, a standardised mode of co-activity. Some institutions are repetitive, i.e., religious and some are contingent in nature, i.e., marriage, law, etc. Aim content of the institutions do constitute their qualitative character. Elements of any institution represent relatively self-contained modes of action realising relatively self-contained aims. Elements in an institution work in two ways : (1) they require each other for the realisation of their several aims and so fall into a 'functional' unit, (2) they also fit or subserve as part purposes and part actions. There are political or economic institutions. They may be classified as follows:

Operative: Somatic; Economic; and Recreational

Regulative: Aesthetic; Scientific; Religious; Educational; Political; Legal; and Kinship

The term 'somatic' is intended to account for all standardised mode of action, whose aims bear specifically on the phases and facts of individual physical existence, such as sex, age, treatment of disease, circumcision and the like. Beaker-Weise speak of 'operative' institutions, which are expected to render a definite service to the society in the institutional capacity. According to Nadel, the 'regulative' institutions bear upon the operation of other institutions, it achieves its purpose or task in enabling the purpose and task of other institutions to be achieved, so that the regulative institution does not merely represent the 'moulds and channels' of behaviour but safeguards them. The relationship between grouping and institutions is very close. They are interdependent on each other. Grouping are visible only in the institutionalised modes of co-activity. The latter appear as the rights and obligations vested in or incumbent upon the individuals in virtue of their membership, either as modes of action reserved for the members of the group or as modes of action generally valid, but typically modified when occurring between group members. All socio-cultural behaviours form and perpetuate by interactions between :

(1) grouping and institution,

(2) grouping and grouping and

(3) institution and institution.

All groupings and institutions may be classified in the following way : (a) those in the forms of social morphology, (b) those in the form of social control, (c) those related to social process and (d) those related to social pathology.

For understanding the social-cultural behaviours in a given community, the groupings and institutions may be studied for three angles mainly : (1) From cohesive point of view, i.e., structural or organisational levels, (2) From conflicting point of view, i.e., from the levels of social stratification and (3) From the view of social process, i.e., culture change. Here, at present, we shall know how to observe societies for social-cultural understanding from structural or organisational level: Social relations and behaviours in general are found in all societies. But among Indian communities, we differentiate one society from the other by labelling them with particular names as Bengali, Oriya, Pir, Pathan, Santal, Toda, etc. Therefore, each must have some specialised social-cultural behaviour over general behaviours which gives respective name. To understand this the social-cultural anthropologist uses conceptual tools namely social structure and social organisation. Structural study deals with the social relations which seems to be of critical importance for the behaviour of members of the society, so that if such relations were not in operation, the society could not be said to exist in that form.

II

Culture is the sum total of human behaviour—verbal and non-verbal and its products—material and non-material. It is very often referred to as the life of people which have their own culture. Culture is also used to convey various meanings in a general way. One uses culture to convey the social charm and intellectuals excellence. So Arnold has said of culture as sweetness and light. Some uses the term culture elite for the intellectual leader of a society. The sociologists MacIver and Sorokin have used the term culture for the moral, spiritual and intellectual attainments of man.

Sanskriti is a Sanskrit term for culture. The term Sanskriti is derived from *Sanskar*, meaning—ritual performance. When one is born, he or she goes through various ritual performances as a result of which he or she is accepted into the various roles like that of an adult or an old or in other words we can describe, man who in the course of his or her life performs and accepts various roles. The state of collective life through which he or she has to go by the performances of various ritual Sanskara is Sanskriti. So Sanskriti is a process of refinement from one stage of life to another.

The anthropologists have used the term 'culture' in different ways. Tylor was the first anthropologist who defined "culture is that complex whole, which includes knowledge, belief, art, morals, law, customs and any other capabilities acquired by man as a member of a society". Here he has getting emphasis on the social heritage and gift of a society to an individual. "I am inclined to say that heredity and learning from a group are the process by which the behaviour of organism is determined" (Tylor, 1871). In man, the heredity contributes such behaviour of sucking and swallowing—being a biological process of transmission. While the behaviour like speaking the language or wearing a cloth is learned from others—a social process of transmission based on the capacity of man to learn. Transmission of behaviour by learning is found among the animal world, but the absence of speeches among them, however, limits the amounts of acquisition. Man alone has his acquisition.

Redfield defines culture "as an organised body of conventional understanding—manifest in art and artifact, which persisting through tradition characterises a human group". Summing up both Tylor and Redfield's views on culture, it can be said that Tylor has emphasized on capabilities acquired by man as a member of society; While Redfield's points stand for persisting through tradition —the important factor in this acquisition through tradition is the ability to learn from the group. But Lowie meant culture as the whole of social tradition.

Malinowski has pointed out that social heritage consists of both material and non-material parts. According to him, the culture is the total way of life and the instruments—mental, social, and material of which this way is made. On the one hand, one has social culture and on the other material culture. This view has been taken and modified by Bidney who has defined culture as the products of agrofacts, artifacts, sociofacts, and mentifacts. This means that culture is the product of cultivation, industry, social organisation and language, religion, art, etc. Radcliffe-Brown like Malinowski has taken the instrumental and humanistic view of culture but he regards culture as cultivation—

the process of handing down and acquiring tradition as a result of which society exists.

Linton, Kluckhohn and Kroeber have said of culture on the plain of subjective nature of human understanding. According to Linton, culture is an abstraction from the reality which is the actual human behaviour. He used the term, social heredity for culture. Kluckhohn describes culture as a way of thinking, feeling and action and Gilling makes it more clear that culture is not activity but its patterning. He notes for a culture as each group, each society, has a set of behaviour patterns, which are more or less common to the members, which have passed down from generation to generation and taught to children and which are liable to change. These common patterns are called culture. Benedict stresses on the patterns of culture and not its content. Kroeber has said that culture includes speech, beliefs, customs, arts and technologies ideals and rules. That in short is what we learn from other men, from our elders or the past plus what we may add to it. According to Green, culture is the socially transmitted system of idealised ways in knowledge, practice and belief. Along with the artifacts that knowledge and practice produce and maintain as they changed in time. Bose, N.K. speaks of culture as crystallised phase of man's life activities. It includes certain forms of acquisition, closely associated with particular objects and institution. Habitual attitudes of mind transferable from one person to another with the aid of mental images conveyed through speech symbols.

Language is the vehicle by which culture is transmitted. Man can inhabit present, past and future by language, i.e., he can built on what he has got from the past and transmit the present with additions to the future.

Records are made and preserved on stones, fire bed clay and metals from the very early days of mankind. Culture can accumulate little by way of knowledge and technology. It becomes the civilisation only when written language comes into existence.

All cultures—primitive or modern, whether hunting, pastoral, or agricultural pattern contain the same types of economy, education, land, folklore, song and institution in a sequence of organisational complexity. Cultural universality is also expressed in similarity in function. This is based on two factors :

(i) Man being a biological species, his food, clothing, shelter, family life, etc., may all vary. But they represent the universal and basic need.

(ii) Survival of man in all places and time; his economy, social control, education, political organisation, religious beliefs and practices, etc., basic points are universal, but differences may be noted between a developed and an underdeveloped society.

From Tylor's definition of culture, it is evident that culture consist of commonly accepted and expected ideas, attitudes, values, and habits of individuals which they learn in connection with the social living. For the individual in his early years of life, culture is an aid to learning to get on more effectively in the world. Each new generation learns how to adjust to the physical and social world mainly from their progenitors. Gradually this new generation passes on to the next generation what it has learnt from the previous one, and what he has added to the cultural whole. Young and Mack, have used three words—*shared, learned* and *behaviour* for culture. Behaviour includes thinking, feeling and action. So any behaviour is a part of culture only when it is shared by members of a group. If only one person uses a neck-tie among the Santals, then this behaviour is not a part of Santal culture. Most of the Bengalis touch their elders, feet when they go outside (at a distant place). This behaviour is shared, and is a part of Bengali culture. By learned behaviour one means more than attitudes and the ways of acting, which are formerly and consciously taught. Any behaviour which is socially acquired that comes through participation in a human group is learned. Of course, certain behaviour is determined by the inheritance. Such behaviour is not cultural. Hunger for food, is not culturally learned, but thought of fried rice or sweets as satisfying or bitter vegetables as repulsive is acquired and is a part of culture.

It is a difficult problem to note the importance of culture as a determinant of human behaviour. One is more likely to overemphasise the effects of heredity or the physical environment then is to recognise how a large portion of his behaviour is composed of shared ways of doing things, to learn in a social environment. Every man likes to think of himself as a quite unusual individual. Still he needs to look about others at the kinds of food eaten, types of clothing worn, forms of greeting used and many other components of culture with respect to uniqueness. The differences which one notes are small within the ways of behaviour expected and accepted in his society. The tests in clothing and most of the behaviour are shared and learned. These are in large parts of culture. In short, it can be said that culture is a precipitated of human society. It is shared and learned behaviour. Man is the only creation of the God that possess culture, the two most significant features of which are language and tools.

Cultural Trait

A cultural trait is a distinguishable unit form of certain traditional ways of actions and of feeling, centrally around objects which may be tangible or intangible. Each isolable element which enters into the composition of a trait is called an *element.* For example, a good number of cultural elements have clustered around rice—the principal foodstuff of Bengal. They consist of material traits like yoke, husking machine (*Dhenki*), ceremonial elements like caste rules and habitual actions connected with technical processes of ploughing, sowing, reaping, and also a number of magical beliefs and practices. Each of these isolable and irreducible component is called an element; while all the elements taken as a whole are set to form as a *trait.* Both trait and element are component units of culture.

Difference between Cultural Trait and Element

1. Trait is bigger and at the same time a complex unit of culture, when it is compared with an element; on the contrary, an element is the smallest isolable and irreducible unit of culture.

2. A trait can be traced when a number of elements combine together giving rise to a bigger traceable unit, while an element can be traced by dividing a trait into a number of smallest isolable, irreducible which are component units of the trait.

3. A number of elements go to form a simple trait.

These are the distinguishing factors between cultural trait and culture complex.

Culture Complex

Traits are seldom observed in life as independent units, when units are linked together to function is called culture complex. As for example—kicking a football combines with many units of behaviour to make the complex by which we know as football game; head-hunting or riding on horse back also illustrate culture complex.

Culture Centre

Culture centre or culture focus (foci) are the sources from which any new culture comes out. Central part of culture area is the central point of dispersal or centre of influence. As for example, rice eating in a particular place or rice eating in earlier days' is now being supplemented by wheat eating which is now becoming prominent.

Culture Area

Area concept represents to order the data in terms of spatial distribution rather than classification derived from the form or function. The areas in which similar cultures are found are called culture areas, such as south-east India as rice eaters and north-west India as wheat eaters.

Dynamic Nature of Culture

The nature of culture is not static but dynamic, i.e., it is subjected to change. No culture in this world is found to be static in nature. One can illustrate the dynamic nature of such changes both from preliterate as well as literate communities. Many tribes have been found to change their cultural pattern due to contacts with urban people.

Industrialisation effects will be sufficient to look at the dynamic aspects of culture. Due to sudden changes, a dynamic aspect of culture is observed among many tribal peoples in their social units and institutions. The earlier joint family concept is being replaced by nuclear families. Thus by change of only one aspect of culture, sometimes the whole way of life gets changed, i.e., in customs, beliefs, or in every social matrix the dynamic aspect of culture is observed. The Americans have completely changed the way of life of the *Azandis* by force.

With the change of environment, the culture of a population is also changing for adapting in a new particular environment. People invented different techniques and technologies. When that environment is changed compulsarily, the technology of people must also change. In some cases, the environment forces to the change of technologies. For example, with the increase in population, the underdeveloped technologies cannot produce sufficient food, so for producing sufficient food output the technology of the group must change.

Consequently, the hoe and digging stick of the primitive people are replaced by plough cultivation. Again with the development, plough cultivation is replaced by tractors and other scientific methods. In doing so, different tribes have changed their occupations—the shifting cultivation to wet cultivation, the food gatherers and hunters have changed to agriculturists and domestic animal rearing tribes. So culture is continuously changing from the very beginning. Thus it can be said that dynamic aspect of culture is observed both by force and inovation.

There are other factors which exert change of culture. In some cases, the environment forces to change their culture. The Marings of Manipur practiced shifting cultivation in their earlier days. Now they have abandoned it, because they are busy in clearing their forests, one after another which affect the rainfall. Now they have migrated to the plains and practice wet and plough cultivations. Thus the environment brings a change of the culture. Again in some cases, the introduction of more efficient and more useful materials brings in the change of culture. For example, with the advent of automobilcs, all the carriages drawn by animals seem to have lost their importance.

III

In anthropology, the term civilisation signifies wide range of conceptions. Presently, the civilisational study offers a method and scope to understand the complex social-cultural process of large scale pre-industrial aggregates of societies in space and in time. Epistemologically, it means the study of the formulation and maintenance of a world-view or cosmology that generates unity in the diverse social structures. Within that unity, varied social-cultural process of diversified societies set in different geographical condition operate.

Kroeber's model (1944) of macroscopic, diachronic and cultural study of civilisation, theoretically, offers no scope to understand the process of civilisation from microscopic emperical situation. On the other hand, Radfield's model (1956) of microscopic, synchronic and socio-cultural study of civilisation conceives two structural dichotomy 'societal structure' and 'cultural structure', whereas the former one maintains wide range of social network within a region, the cultural structure transcends the regional boundary. The cultural structure of a civilisation, again, has been conceived dichotomically with the 'great tradition' — the tradition of urban literates and cultural specialists and the 'little tradition'—the tradition of rural non-literate mass. In a civilisation process, these two traditions not only maintain the distinctive autonomy in cultural sphere, but they are in constant interaction with each other.

Later, a host of anthropologists applied Radfield's model in Indian context. The contribution of a few of them is very significant. The process of interaction between the two traditions, however, received a conceptual treatment—the formulation of the process of 'universalisation' through which the local cultural materials are recognised as pan-Indian and 'parochialisation' through which the cultural ideas become localised, by Marriott (1966). Singer has formulated the concept 'cultural performances' through which the great tradition of a civilisation is maintained by both the specialists and commoners (1972). With special reference to Indian history, Cohn (1971) observes that Indian civilisation is segmented by region and major religious tradition, yet, it never developed a single orthodoxy for any period of time. The diversity due to regional segmentation is transcended by the unity of the civilisation, observes Marriott and Cohn (1968). That unity exists through the cultivation of cultural specialists living in the centres, great and small, who are further connected with thousands of the villages by cultural link, thus overrule the regional diversity.

The quest for anthropology of Indian civilisation, in the Indian anthropology was initiated by Bose. His 'Hindu Social Structure' model (1948) was essentially a social historical approach to the caste structure and organisation as an economic system of Indian civilisation. The structure remains, however, integrated through the communication of the Brahmanism, its ideas and ideals among the socially heterogeneous caste groups. Saraswati resolves that the integrity in Indian civilisation lies with the religion, specially with the Hindu ascetics and sacred complex (1970, 1978).

From the view point of contextual reality, here, the question whether 'Indian civilisation' and 'Hindu civilisation' are co-terminous, cannot be avoided. The term Hindu was being used by the Muslim invaders during the medieval period (Majumdar, 1977; Karve, 1977). The term had been derived from the name Sindhu river as a result of regular sound shifting by the Persian and Greek traders engaged in trading at Sindu river basin during historical period (Majumdar, 1977; Basham, 1984). Radhakrishnan suggests the territorial significance of the term Hindu, which had originally no creditable significance (1954). Radhakrishnan (1954) and Renou (1961) refer Indian civilisation as that of Hindu which flourished on Indian soil. Nikkam (1967) and Brown (1966) are of the opinion that Indian civilisation is the product of Hindu civilisation.

From Bose's writings, it appears that as early as 1929 he had already decided that his subject matter was not tribal or local systems of caste in villages, but the total structure of Indian civilisation. During 1942-45, as a political prisoner under the British government, he gave a series of features on the structure of Hindu society to the fellow political prisoners. These lectures, however, have formed the basis of his Bengali book; *Hindu Samajer Garan*, (1949) (Structure of Hindu Society). This was written quite a few years before "*Comparison of Civilisations*" became a proper subject of study for anthropologists under the leadership of Robert Redfield.

Starting with a prelude quoting *Chaitanya Charitamrita* at a great length, he presented his views historically. Into this broad canvas of time, he brings in many dimensions of Indian social structure and social processes. The tribal enclaves and their absorptions, the dual themes of self-sufficiency of village communities and their broader links with kinship; fairs and pilgrim centres; norms of sacred and secular life in the ancient texts, social movements in the medieval period in response to Islam; the impact of British rule and the emerging economy on Indian society, particularly on the caste system. Anthropological study of Indian civilisation involves a combination of many perspectives—analysis of classical and medieval texts, administrative records particularly of land tenure and studies of villages, individual castes' associations and the wider social networks of the civilisation in kinship, fairs, pilgrim, centres, and so on. The historical situation in which the classical *Varna-Jati*—system of social order came into being will not be repeated in modern times. It will also suit our times, for the population of India has increased manifold and land per capita has diminished considerably. Yet, if we discover some values and social designs in the traditional system which has relevance for the modern time, it will be unwise not to utilise them in solving our contemporary problems. For, in the ultimate analysis, the human-kind cannot be set apart by time and space.

According to N. K. Bose, "Indian civilisation encouraged diversity of cultures, while in its economic organisation, it tried to weave all communities into a network of interdependent, but distinct, entities" (1971).

Bose feels that the creative potentialities of the traditional structure of Indian civilisation cannot be properly assessed, if the observations are only limited to the post-medieval and recent phase of recession of the civilisation. The carrier of civilisation has also to be studied in a phase of expansion and confidence.

Although, Bose has been a persistent student of Indian civilisation, he has not made any conscious effort to distinguish the concept of "civilisation from that of culture". He has, however, thrown some interesting hints on the general characteristics of a civilisation.

In a particular case, Bose states that the civilisation of Bengal cannot be merely defined in terms of spatial and temporal continuity of tradition. "In this formidable adventure of cultural reorganisation, Bengali culture has always been in the process of becoming, instead of merely being. This tendency to become something is the characteristic of any civilisation. When there is a continuity between aspirations, we regard the two as belonging to one civilisation".

Thus according to Bose the study of civilisation is essentially a study of the inner moods, that is, matters of the mind, responding to the changing life experiences of a people.

Indian civilisation in its totality appreciated from one point of view, how the Indian in the highest flights of their thought and being transcended the bounds of local temporisation, i.e., of culture, as it grew up due to the emergencies of a situation. It thus became a historical in the end.

An endeavour may be made to describe in broad outline the ruling ideas working behind Indian or Hindu civilisation—a productive organisation. To describe in broad outline of the Indian or Hindu civilisation, a productive organisation may be built up on monopolistic, hereditary guilds of farmers and craftsmen and even of soldiers, which will encourage to follow its own *dharma* and by means of the complementary service of these *dharmas* that the life of the people as a whole will sustain. The regulatory power lays in the hands of the king; and it was his duty to see to it that each guild followed its own prescribed duties. He did so with the advice of the colleges of Brahmans, which were either located in famous centres of learning or of pilgrimage. These centres might remain in temples or *muths*, or in *ashramas* or *akhras* or village settlements of Brahmans, founded by the rulers of the land.

There was a superstructure guiding the religious and cultural life of the community as a whole. Each small component, called a *jati*, was left free to pursue its own rites and ceremonies, so long as it did not militate against the moral codes of Brahmanical society. If a tribe absorbed the Hindu social organisation, originally practising human sacrifice, they were encouraged to give it up and replace by the sacrifice of a buffalo or a goat, or even that of a substance like a gourd. The *shraddha* or respect of a *jati* for its own religious beliefs was not to be uprooted, but only modified. And this is how, in the course of a long history, Hinduism became a confederation of many beliefs and practices. The Hindus' belief that the migrations of individual soul, i.e., from one birth to another and belief in spiritual progress towards greater truth until he reaches the highest phase, like the heavens from where all frequents of truth by which men ordered their lives on the earth below appeared, each to be true in its own context.

It is not necessary for us to evaluate the central core of ideas in Hindu civilisation from a different point of view. Through ages, Hinduism has tried to promote ideas and spiritual exercises designed to promote the growth of every individual soul in this direction. Individuals and communities have been encouraged to remain in their special worlds with the result that even if the economic and social organisation of caste have suppressed individualism at one level. Hindus have remained loyal to individualism of another kind, and never allowed themselves to be fused into one uniform mass.

India in the course of its long history of three thousand years or so, we notice certain broad points of strength and weakness lying within. Ever since the Afghan, Tartar and Moghul invaders professing Islam came to the land, it had been proved again and again that the political structure of India was very weak in self-defence. In it, the defence of the state become exclusive business of several castes but not all the inhabitants of the state. Many cultures and religions that existed side by side with one another, but the feeling of distinctness which was thus encouraged have failed when there was need of combining the people into one "nation" for the purposes of defence.

Caste has been held largely responsible factor for the absence of a sense of national unity. The multiplicity of faiths in India, her variegated ways of life, with different kinds of food and dress, her many languages have also been equally blamed for our lack of the sense of national unity.

Let us observe each civilisation and its attainments in the perspective of history. And then we shall be able to realise that each little company of men has contributed its share to the common pole of human civilisation, for the total achievements of the human race.

Anthropological View of Indian Civilisation

Historians and philosophers compare civilisations by the excellence of their attainments in various creative fields, or by the power which they have developed in preserving or expanding the influence of their civilisation upon their communities. In contrast, an anthropologist who usually deals with simpler and smaller communities has a less difficult task to perform. For instance, if there are two communities, which live principally by agriculture and do not depend very much upon trade, he might compare how many persons each can support on a square mile of similar land by means of its productive organisation. Of course, in order to make comparison valid, it is also necessary to assume that the standard of living assumed by each has been brought down to a nearly common and comparable level. From this point of view, let us examine the kind of culture which prevails among some of India's indigenous people and the population of our villages, and how they have interacted with one another in the past, and are doing so even in our own times.

In India, it was possible for the Hindus to build up a social system and a civilisation based normatively upon hereditary guilds of specialists in which competition was discouraged, and mutual assistance plus conspicuous expenditure through rites and ceremonies and gifts was encouraged. With regard to the religious faiths and rituals, there was a tolerance of a very special kind. On account of these, and inspite of the fact that caste was also a kind of class division, which divided the population into those who toiled and those who primarily lived on the toils of others, caste did succeed in enduring over centuries through many vicissitudes of history. The civilisation which was built up in India should be examined from a truly scientific and historical point of view(Bose, 1972).

The dominant characteristic of the concept is that Indian civilisation has tried in the past to bring together many people and cultures within the ambit of a common civilisation. What strikes us is that caste was built up with one intention in view, while "nationalism" was built up with another central intention in Europe in recent times. Even in earlier periods, when much of Europe was under the sway of either imperial Rome or of the Holy Roman Empire, the intention was to build up as much of uniformity as possible. In contrast, Indian civilisation encouraged diversity of cultures, while in its economic organisation, it tried to weave all the communities into a network of interdependent, but distinct entities.

Moreover, each civilisation had developed its own strengths and weaknesses. Indians do not feel hurt when one part of India differs from another in the patterns of food, dress, language or domestic architecture. Many Indian thinkers, during the nineteenth and twentieth centuries have deplored the material weakness of the Indian people as a nation. They have wished that India should develop a common language and a common script, so that she can become a unified and powerful nation in the modern technical sense of the term. That nation has been unified since 1947 by common political and economic ties, but according to them, much more is necessary; culturally all differences should be obliterated as far as possible.

In our passion for national 'unification', let us not in a hurry throw away something from our historical experiences, which may be of permanent value. India can take an equal pride in having made original contributions of its own about the peaceful co-existence of many people and many cultures. These lessons drawn from the historical experience need not be scorned just because they have become rusty, clothed in routinised religious rituals and thus become uncreative. With the knowledge of modern science, with our powers of analysis and discrimination, we can take off the rust from whatever is best in Indian civilisation, and make the life of human kind richer and more fruitful in the creative sense, than it has ever been in the past.

In studying civilisation Redfield proposed for the study of Great and Little tradition. He also introduced the term "Cultural Specialists", for such a group of people who function as intermediary between great and little tradition. He also coined the term 'cultural media' from Milton Singer which represents song, dance, performing folk art and drama etc., through such channels where these specialists may able to communicate the mass and thus a continuity is established between the two traditions. Redfield was of opinion that a civilization has both great regional scope and historic depth. Basing on these idea from Redfield and Singer, the Indian scholars as well as foreigners also initiated their effort to understand Indian civilization. Singer applied the concept of Redfield in his Madras city study with especial reference to cultural specialists in Indian situation. Among the notable scholars in this arena were Vidyarthi who developed the concept of 'sacred complex' for studying the pilgrim centre as a dimension of Indian civilization. Marriott and Cohn developed the concepts of 'Network and centres' to study the channels of integration of Indian civilization. Saraswati's concept of *Nilakantha syndrome*, '*Măryada*, *Parampara* are also another dimension to understand the changing scenario of Indian civilization. Dube's multiple tradition model signifies that Indian civilization is composed of six traditions, namely, classical, national, regional, local, western and local sub-cultural. All of those should be studied in rural and urban context. Sinha's historical and interactional model to study Indian civilization is actual interaction between communities both on synchronic and diachronic level. According to Karve Indian civilization is understood basing on four distinctive regions and on four distinctive factors (historical, linguistic, cultural, etc.) Roy Burman introduced the concept of nation and sub-nation to understand Indian social system in terms of social-political process. While Danda's composite culture model reveals that Indian civilization is of composite character of social system. He suggested Indian civilization is a product of interaction many great and little traditions.

4 Political Organisation

Politics, as the legitimate or organised use of authority in a society which is, however, deeply related with law and order as well as social control of a society. The anthropologists who studies this area of social behaviour is interested not only in the formal definitions of rules, but in the way people actually act, whether they conform to the rules or not. Since laws are a guide for an appropriate conduct in a particular society, we can learn from them what kinds of actions people consider to be contrary to their values and the degree of punishment can also indicate the extent of transgression. In our own society we can get a clear picture of our prescribed norms and values and through which we able to know the action which is legal, illegal, offence and crime, etc. The same kinds of insights can help the anthropologist to understand something about the values shared by people in other societies like tribals and other illiterate ethnic groups.

Despite the absence of rulers, centralized decision-making bodies, written legal codes and law enforcement agencies, we find in one way or another every society engages in political activity.

By political organisation one means the institutions

by which laws and orders are maintained in a society as well as with neighbouring communities. Thus political organisation stands for the legal institutions by which judicial rights of the people are safeguarded and the judicial obligations are enforced on them. Among the tribal people this varies, that is, it varies from hunting, food gathering society to settled cultivators. There is no judicial institution like court of the modern urban system while they have their own jati panchayat and village panchayat or council where their elder members are the members and all sorts of disputes are discussed and settled in their traditional council. Each ethnic groups have their own sanction law which is otherwise called as Customary Law.

Law is codified form of sanctions prevalent in the society. Sanction is the social force which brings or impels a person to behave in conformity as prescribed by a given society. Broadly the social sanction includes suggestion, persuasion, encouragement, bravery, reward, etc., for those who follow prescribed behaviour in a society while at the same time it also includes restraint, supress, disgrace, condemnation, crime and even award punishment to those who tries to deviate from the mainstream.

Among the social sanction there is positive sanction which includes observance of social standards as approved by the community. There is a belief that ancestors and spiritual beings are pleased by offering of various rites. In the present day many charitable organisation of some specific ethnic group are making hospitals, schools and passengers shed in the bus stopage in a metropolitan cities, etc., which brings their position as well as social activity in the society. Many primitive people of America spend their surplus food during festive occasion and also destroy their valuable in a fire and thereby their position is raised in the society. This ritual is often known as *potlach.*

Apart from positive sanction there is negative sanction which means non-observance of social standards, that is, when a person violates code of conduct in a society, is punished.

(i) *Unorganised:*

(a) There is supernatural sanction. The norms are guided by the supernatural power. The tribal people believes that if one violates their existing norms, he will be punished by the supernatural forces like blood vomiting, fell ill, or their cattle will die, etc.

(b) *Automatic Sanction*—It is defined as a punishment by the act itself, that is, a breach of taboo.

(c) *Ritual*—A guilty person is identified by some magical performance by the magician. By the act of magician or sorcerer the guilty person will be harmed and then he is identified before the villagers.

(ii) *Organised Sanction*—It consists of oath, ordeal, trial, weired guild, etc.

(a) *Oath*—It means a kind of promise. Among some tribes of Chotanagpur plateau a man before giving his observations in front of panchayat is asked to take an oath on tiger's skin or in the name of *bonga.* Among them oath is taken for the decision of a dispute. They have a faith that a guilty person never dares in telling a lie after taking oath.

(b) *Ordeal*—It is a kind of test in supernatural

power. It is done with water, fire and charcoal. We may observed from the Ramayana the ordeal test of Sita when she walked into the fire but remained unaffected and thus she proves herself as *Pativarta* (only devoted and attached to her husband Rama). Among the Oraons tribe there is a custom that when a theft takes place, the suspected persons are asked to keep burning charcoal on the palm, the person who unable to tolerate the pain for a moment is considered to be guilty.

(c) *Weired-guild*—It is the punishment through compensation.

(d) *Trial*—Tribal people are endogamous but practice clan exogamy. When a person violates it he is asked to present before village panchayat for trial. The punishment are as out casting and as a result social intercourse with other neighbouring groups are tabooed. Infact, trials are more rationalistic procedures of inquiry in which witness give testimony and evidence is submitted. The trial is also a method of adjudication or a decision in a dispute. Method of adjudication are found in every society—they may be 'formal' or 'informal'.

A society's formal means of social control are often the most overt, they are not the only procedures for reducing conflicts and settling disputes. Every society has a range of both formal and informal mechanisms of social control. The norms that underlie social control mechanisms are often ambiguous. Infact, mechanisms of social control do serve to reduce deviance but actually they do not eradicate it. A certain amount of deviance is as essential to the survival of a society.

5 PRIMITIVE RELIGION

Religion is an important or even an essential part of the social machinery as are morality and law part of the complex system by which human beings are enabled to live together in an orderly arrangement of social relations. Religion consists of beliefs and practices. Durkheim defines religion a united system of beliefs and practices related to sacred things which unites into a single moral community called a church or sect, all those who adhere to them. According to Tylor, religion is the belief in supernatural beings. According to Brown, religion is the bodies of erroneous beliefs of certain ideas on the one hand and on the other illusory ritual practices and certain observances (rites). Religion to Brown is the product of false psychology, for example, it is sometimes held that funeral and mourning rites are the result of a belief in soul surviving death. It is religious action or the need of action that controls or determines the belief. The actions themselves are symbolic expressions of sentiments. Religion is everywhere an expression in one form or another of a sense of dependence on a power outside ourselves, a power which we may speak of as a spiritual or supernatural power. In maintaining social cohesion and equilibrium, the religion plays a most important part. The religion is an intrinsic part of the constitution of society. For Malinowski (1951) religion is the integrative needs of man in society. To him, the essential significance of religion was that it gives man courages to face the world and in particular the inevitability of death.

Religion is instinctive to man. Man being the only religious being distinguishes him from animals. As and when he was compelled to face natural hardships and dangers like storms, floods, epidemics, famines, deluge, dreaded animals, etc., man has looked up to some invisible power for assistance, motivation, strength and help. Man also tried to realise this intangible power for reasons such as to obtain salvation from the sorrows and transience, birth, death and old age.

So far we know all societies have possessed beliefs which can be labelled under the term religion. These belief vary from region to region and again from culture to culture. Whatever, the variety of beliefs in things supernatural, we may define religion as any set of attitudes, beliefs, and practices pertaining to supernatural power, whether the power be a kind of forces, gods, spirits, demons or ghosts. Moreover, to consider one affair either due to supernatural power or subject to the laws of nature—varies from society to society. Such as, some illness in modern society may be identified due to virus attack while among primitive society is thought to result from supernatural forces and that again identified by their magician or sorceror and thus it forms a part of religious belief.

Herbert Spencer develops the theory of ghost worship by dealing elaboratedly with the primitive idea of life, death, resurrection, soul, spirit, the other world and the cult of the ghost. Spencer finds that some notion of existence beyond death, however vague, is almost universal. From this belief comes the idea of soul propitiation, not only at the time of funeral but it continues. Infact, this idea in due course develops the worship of ancestors. From this Spencer concludes that ancestor worship is the root of every religion and all other forms, namely, idol worship, fetish worship, animal, plant and nature worship, etc.

Ancestors may be of different forms:

(i) In primitive culture we find the ancestor is represented by the Supreme Being. This form of Supreme Being is found among the Pygmies of Africa, some Australian aborigines, natives of California, *bonga* among Santal, *dhartimai* among the Parhaiya—a Scheduled Tribe of Chotanagpur.

(ii) In the boomerang culture among Australian aborigines and Africa the conception of the ancestor is somewhat different. Here we find a single figure, the first father. He is the first mortal, risen from the dead and is often equated with the moon.

(iii) If we look into our Indian society we find that the first father no longer receives worships, but a number of dead ancestors are worshipped. Among the Mongolians, Turkish nomads we may observe that the father of the race has acquired the same cult as the Supreme Being.

(iv) Ancestor worship may take the form of totemism. It is found in India, Australia, Africa, U.S.A. etc.

(v) The ancestor worship in matrilineal society instead of father the tribal mother is identified with the moon or with the mother earth.

Religion is a universal and pervasive in situation in

human society. Religion may be broadly defined as a system of beliefs, emotional attitudes and practices by means of which a group of people attempt to cope with the ultimate problems of human life. The great religions of the world contains five basic elements:

1. Belief in supernatural power.
2. Belief in the holy.
3. Ritual.
4. Acts defined as sinful.
5. Some methods of salvation or nirvana.

1. *Belief in Supernatural Power*

The first basic element of religion is the belief that there are supernatural powers—powers outside of man and his observable world which influence human life and control all natural phenomena. Some call these supernatural forces god, other call them gods. There are even others who do not call them by any name, they simply recognize them as forces in their universe to which men must adjust themselves. In other words, belief in the non-sensory, superempirical world is the first element of religion.

2. *Belief in the Holy*

The holy or sacred constitutes the heart of religion. There are certain things which are regarded as holy or sacred. Sacred things are symbols. They symbolize the things of the unseen, superempirical world, they symbolize certain sacred things tangible realities. When a Hindu worships a cow, he worships it not because of the kind of animal. The cow is trust because of a host superempirical characteristics which this animal is imagined represent.

3. *Ritual*

Religious ritual is the active side of religion. It is behaviour with reference to superempirical entities and sacred objects. It includes any kind of behaviour, prayers, hymns, reedal, recitations and other forms of reference usually performed with other people and in public. It can include singing, dancing, weeping, crawling, fasting, etc.

4. *Acts Defined as Sinful*

Religion defines certain acts as profane and sinful. There are certain moral tenents which are explained as having a supernatural origin. It is believed that the powers of other world support and cherish these principles. The violation of these principles not only creates man's sense of guilt, it may bring upon him the disfavour of the supernatural power.

5. *Some Methods of Salvation*

Redemption or a method of salvation constitutes the fifth basic element of religions. It may take various forms. The Hindu seeks release from the bondage of Karma, which is the joy or suffering. He undergoes as a result of his actions in their life. He may accomplish it by recognizing the inadequacy of the senses, by his striving for the ultimate goal and by practicing inner spiritual contemplation. The Buddhist hopes to attain salvation by being absorbed in the godhead and entering Nirvana. The Christian has a redeemer in Lord Christ, the Son of God who gave His life for man's sins.

In short, religion is the institutionalized set of beliefs. Men hold about supernatural forces. Beliefs are formalized and regularized in the temples or church, etc. Ideas are developed in regard to the nature of the supernatural power, the methods of acquiring it, the beings who possess it and the appropriate regard in

Religion and supernaturalism are closely interrelated. The structure of religion is as follows:

RELIGION

- FORMS
  1. Animism
  2. Animatism
  3. Naturalism
  4. Totemism
  5. Supreme Being
  6. Mana
  7. Magic
- PRACTICES
  - Individual
    - Rites de passage (Rituals associated with life cycle)
    - Domestic (Ceremonies puja, etc.)
  - Communal
- PRACTITIONERS
  - Priests (Objects and practices of everyday life)
  - Magicians (Shaman, witchcraft doctor)

which they are to be hold. Appropriate rituals are established and special leaders (priests) are developed for religious life. In this way religious complex develops and religion affects familial, educational, governmental, recreational and social activity.

Tribal religion is the most primitive form of religion. The following are the important types of belief of Indian tribal religion.

(i) *Animism.* Animism is the belief in spiritual beings. It is made up of two components: first, concerning the souls of individuals capable of continued existence after death; second, concerning other spirits, superior to man and upto the rank of powerful deities. Animism in its full development includes the belief in the existence of bodyless souls capable of controlling deities and subordinate spirits. According to Risley tribal religion is animism. The tribal people believe in the presence of supernatural powers at the top of hills, flooded rivers, big and old trees, etc. They try to please these powers by means of different types of propitiations and worships. An important type of animism is ancestral worship which is found among the Santals and Oraons. The Santals worship deities of family and village. Among the Korwa tribe there is a goddess of crop. Among the Bhatra tribe of Bastar they have rain deity—Bhima-Bhimi. The tribal people try to please their deity by offering flowers, fruits and alcoholic drinks and sacrificing birds and animals. The Khonds of Orissa have a belief in quadruple souls. In the Hindu society also we find animistic belief. Such as setting up lights on the tops of long bamboo poles in the month of Kartick (October-November) to light the spirits of our forefathers to Heaven through the dark regions of chaos.

The word animism was first coined by Tylor and according to him, animism is the ground work of the philosophy of religion from the savegery to the civilization. According to Tylor animism originated in the attempt of the primitive man to explain dreams and visions, leading to his formation of the idea of the independent ethereal existence of the soul. But Durkheim objects to it on the ground that the complete dissociation of the soul from the body is not to be found in the primitive belief in all its aspects.

(ii) *Animatism.* According to Marett (1909) through his book *The Threshold of Religion*, proposed instead of soul, it is the "nature" which guides the destiny of the primitive people and coined the word *animatism* for understanding primitive religion. Thus, animatism is some impersonal power behind every material object besides the living beings. This impersonal power is worshipped to maintain peace and prosperity in the group. Some of the Chotanagpur tribes of Bihar consider bones, feathers, stone, beads, etc., have some magical powers.

(iii) *Naturalism.* A universal characteristic of tribal religion is to worship of nature, various Indian tribe worships, sun, moon, rivers, mountains, stars, trees and other natural objects. In fact German scholar, Max Müller advocated the theory of *naturalism.*

(iv) *Totemism.* This word derived from American Indian word 'totem'. A totem is a class of material objects which a savage regards with superstitions respect, believing that there exists between him and every member of the class an intimate and altogether special relation. The totem have a special position in Indian tribal religion. Different Indian tribes believe in different types of totems. The totem is considered to be the originater of a particular clan or lineage group of a tribe. It is worshipped and respected everywhere, and its killing and eating is strictly forbidden. Marriages cannot be solemnized in the same totem group as they are believed to have originated from same stock and thus having blood relationship. The name of some totems are as *hansda* (duck), *minz* (a kind of fish), *baghel* (tiger), *kashap* (a tortoise), *ekka* (a tortoise), *kujur* (a kind of creeper), *karketta* (a kind of bird), *tirki* (a bird), *Nag* (snake), *Lakra* (tiger), etc.

(v) *Belief in the Supreme Being.* According to historical school, the development of human cultures may be categorised into four levels—

I. Primitive cultures, food gatherers;

II. Primary cultures, food producers : higher stage of hunting, horticulture and pastorial nomads;

III. Secondary cultures or hoe culture;

IV. Tertiary culture or introduction of plough or settled cultivation.

Belief in the Supreme Being or a kind of power is prevalent in various forms in the aforesaid four levels of various primitive communities (these levels vary according to their degree of development). Among some of the primitive peoples like Andamanese, Semang, South-East Australian Aborigines, there is a belief that the Supreme Being originally lived with them on the earth. But later on being offended by some sinful act of human being 'He' went away to live in the sky. He is often believed as living in the sky and He expresses His anger through thunder-storm. This belief is observed among Semang and Bushman. Sometimes it is found that the Supreme Being is connected with rain as a source of fertility of agricultural land. This belief is prevalent among the Bhatra tribe of Bastar. The empirical study of Indian tribal scenario represent that the Supreme Being have eight attributes, viz., eternity, omnipotence, omniscience, beneficence, creative power, morality, moral codes and moral gurdians. This the Supreme Being is worshipped through prayer, sacrifice and with some religious acts and ceremonies.

(vi) *Magic.* One of the most important feature of tribal religion is faith in magic. Tylor in his book *Primitive Culture* has described magic as a pseudo-science, i.e. false. In *Totemism and Exogamy* (1910) of Frazer too thought of magic as a false science. Magic is a spurious system of abortive art controlling the supernatural thing by some fictitious man called magician. Accordingly, magic may be grouped under two heads namely, immitative or homeopathic magic and sympathetic or contagious magic. Similar thing begets similar object which is known as Homeopathic, i.e., like produces like. While in sympathetic magic is based on law of contactor in the belief that a thing once in contact with a person always in contact. So the magic requires some parts or portions of clothing, pairing of hairs, nails, etc. Magic is the power over power the power of supernatural agencies through the experts called magicians. The efficacy of magic may be thought to depend essentially upon the correct treatment of the substances used including words of magical spells spoken over them independently of assistance from any supernatural being. Thus, magic is a practice designed to manipulate the supernatural forces, while witchcraft is used as an explanation of how or why things happen as they did. Witchcraft can be used to explain unfortunate events.

The evolution of human cultures was postulated by magic, religion and science by Frazer while according to Tylor it was from savagery to barbarism to civilization.

The basic differences between Science and Magic and Religion and Magic are as follows:

Science	*Magic*
1. Science is based on observation and guided by logical explanation.	1. Magic is full of mysterious.
2. Science is product of experiment ⟶ observ ation ⟶ inferences.	2. Magic is primarily tradition oriented.
3. Science is open to all and it is the product of cause and effect relationship	3. Magic is an occult, it is taught through mysterious institution.

According to Beals and Hoijer, "major is a body of techniques and methods for controlling the universe, on the assumption that if certain procedures are followed minutely certain results are inevitable. It presupposes an orderly universe of cause and effect". In the following table the difference between magic and religion are described.

Religion	*Magic*
1. Prevails in modern and advanced societies (settled agriculturist, settled pastoralist, and industrial centre)	1. Prevails in the primitive societies (nomadic, shifting cultivators, hunter-gatherer and nomadic pastoral)
2. Sacred	2. Profane
3. Organised	3. It is fictitious or false which is called as pseudo science.
4. It has three main components Religion: Forms; Practices ↓ Ceremonies, rituals; Practitioner ↓ Priest	4. Broadly divided into sympathetic and Home-opathic or immitative magic.

5. It is performed in certain occasion.	5. It has no such occasion.
6. Religion is meant a propitiation of God or supernatural, i.e., powers superior to man.	6. Magic is the powers which overpowers on power of supernatural agencies which deals with the spirits.
7. Religion is benevolent.	7. Magic is malevolent.
8. Religion is a system of faith and worship based on such a belief.	8. Magic is secret and individual.
9. Religion is social.	9. Magic is anti-social.
10. Religion is performed in one institutions like shrine, temple, church, mosque, pagoda.	10. Magic has no institution like church, temple, etc.
11. Performed by the mediator known as priest.	11. Performed always by the experts called magician.

(vii) *Mana*. It may be designate a type of supernatural power either in a person or in an object and such a set of beliefs was termed as *mana* as used by Melanesian. Mana may be a kind of Supreme Being which is discussed earlier. The term *mana* coined by Codrington during his field work among Melanesians. Majumdar conception of *Bonga* among Ho tribe of Chotanagpur may be equated with *mana*.

The other components of the structure of religion is practice part and practitioners. Infact, the ritual, the action of religion are associated with various ceremonies, worships and life cycle rituals, etc. Where it is performed either individually or communally and these rituals are conducted by specialists like priest and magician such as *ojha, pahan, baiga, sirha*, etc.

The history of religion includes periods of strong resistance to change and periods of radical change. One explanation is that religious practices always originate during periods of stress. The empirical observation from Indian tribes reveals that 'tribal religion' have gradually replaced animism and come very close to broad Hinduism in the country. Infact this phenomena may be observed through N.K. Bose (1941) article on "Hindu Method of Tribal Absorption" where he showed how Hindu cultural trait is borrowed by tribe due to their co-existence with the Hindu.

The primitive tribes of India come in close contact with Hinduism and Christianity as well as urban mode of life to whom they are dependent on their economic sphere, and due to such contact for a prolonged period some of them acquire some Hindu religious traits and code of conduct into their own and some even become ashamed of their past heritage like sorcercy, witchcraft and other black magic, etc. Infact magic and religious aspect of primitive tribes of India are greatly interwoven.

6 Method and Technique

A methodology is the analytical study of methods. Specific studies are examined here as to the procedures adopted, the assumptions made, and the results obtained. The nature of the generalisations, it any, and the explanations, if attempted are also scrutinised.

The object of study in socio-cultural anthropology is human society and human behaviour arising out of human interaction and interrelation. It is concerned with all the happenings to human beings in virtue of their relations to each other.

The unit of study is the behaviour of group of man, that is essentially composed of individual attitudes of living persons which vary from one place to another. The subjects of the observer belong to the same category sharing similar type of life experiences, emotions and feelings, so the methods of approach to the problems vary from other sciences.

In technique, social-cultural anthropologists depend on the personal observation supplemented by records of case histories. He attempts to understand the experience, the norms and pattern of behaviour of people under investigation by staying among them, which takes time.

For explanation and diagnosis, the socio-cultural anthropology depends mainly on comparison or analytic procedure and sometimes on deduction. Thus social-cultural anthropology is a science as its generalisation are based on "controlled comparison" which includes the co-ordination of induction as well as deduction. Subject matter of socio-cultural anthropology (institution, grouping, etc.) in most part functionally depends on or related to one another.

For achieving the above end, the socio-cultural anthropologists employ different methods and techniques for the collection of necessary data. The chief among them are discussed in the following lines.

Before going into detail the authors would like to clarify what are its methods and techniques.

By definition a method implies a goal or an end to be achieved, or, a method is more than an interrelation of a number of techniques. According to Herskovits, (1954) the social-cultural anthropologists insightfully assert that the term method indicates more than those procedures utilised to execute a given research project, whereas a technique is a device, a means or a procedure—verbal or mechanical in nature for collecting and processing the data in the particular context of a scientific enquiry. Some techniques commonly used in social science research are such interviews, case studies observation, etc.

For the collection of anthropological data from the field, the field worker employs various techniques as per suitability. The entire field work procedure may be divided into two parts: (i) collection of data (ii) analysis and writing of report. Broadly, the collection of data is done again in three levels, viz., (a) by observation (b) by conversation like case history, narrative, genealogical, interviews, etc. (c) and by the use of both.

The Techniques of Observation

The entire method is divided into two parts: (a) collection of data and (b) analysis of documents, i.e., collected data. The comparative method forms the basis of cultural or social anthropology. There are certain techniques which are broadly used by the cultural or social anthropologists in collecting the data. The collection of data by direct observation of social reality needs the help of enquires, interviews, questionnaires, etc., in the field. The direct observation can itself be divided into parts, either samples are used to analyse the larger communities, but this does not permit very prefound analysis, or small communities (and even individuals) are observed and this will give in depth what is lost in the previous one. For this the first will be called extensive observation and the second intensive observation. Sometimes, it is difficult to distinguish between them. Some techniques are common to both, although they differ somewhat in their application for example the interview by questionnaire method is used in both the observations.

Direct Extensive Observation

The most popular form of direct extensive observation is by polls—a small sample of a large community is examined and the conclusion drawn from it are generalised. This remains valid, if the sample is really representative.

Questionnaire Method

Hypothetically in order to obtain the full data, a set of questions is prepared and put to the informant, where he answers according to his desire. There are different categories of questions. The fundamental distinction, however, rests on the degree of freedom in the reply. Another important distinction is based on the nature of reply sought. The different categories are as follows:

1. *Open and closed question.* A close question is the one to which *Yes* or *No* opinion are the only possible replies. A open or free question is the one in which the respondent can answer as he likes—here he is not limited to a single alternative. Open and closed questions have exactly the opposite advantage and disadvantages. The former allows a much less superfield inquiry of the attitude and opinion of respondents could be obtained, whereas the latter have the great advantage of being easy to handle; and the interpretation of the result does not present any problems.

Open questions leave sufficient room for subjectivity—in transcribing and interpreting of the replies. In practice, a good questionnaire should include the categories of such questions for all the main problems of investigation.

2. *Questions with a series of alternative.* Here the questions are put with the series of alternative replies.

3. *Evaluative questions.* For example, what is your opinion of the policy of socialist trade unions vis-a-vis the communist trade unions completely approving, qualified disapproval, complete disapproal. Here the informants have evaluative choice.

4. *Questions of fact or about action.* In census questions, the facts are very numerous. The subjects are asked, e.g., the area of land which they form, the number of rooms in their dwellings and the size of the rooms and their income. In opinion polls, there are a certain number of indispensible questions about the

fact-age, sex, profession, habitats, resources, etc. In principle, there is high level of honesty of replies and there are not many refusals to reply. The exceptions are in those cases, where the subject fears that this reply will damage his interest.

5. *Questions about intention and opinion* : There are some questions which include both intention and opinion such as which political party one prefers is a question of the opinion, but the intention can also be recognised.

In questionnaire method, the informant remains under the control of the observer, but the customs or information remaining outside the framework of questions and hypothesis according to which the questions are set, remain unrecorded.

Direct Intensive Observation

Direct extensive observation is conducted on the large and populous communities through representative samples, leading to the extensive observation with profound or sufficient depth. Direct intensive observation is exactly carried out on small groups or even on the individuals. It is therefore not as vide, but has more details in greater depth.

Limitations of Observation Method

Investigators have to stay for pretty longer in the actual area of field and observer the case and incidence. There are some incidents which occur all of a sudden, and are repeated after a longer period such as drought, flood, suicide, marriage, death, election of panchayats, village ceremonies, etc. Sometimes, the observations must be clarified time to time or observation should be supplemented by conversation for better understanding, that calls for—

(i) knowledge of respective language,

(ii) prolonged stay, and

(iii) area of observation should be narrow.

Conversation

This is the method, where the informant is allowed to converse or discuss with the field worker on some topic and from where data is taken. This is of following modes.

Descriptive

This technique is also known as narrative. Narration or description is the most important factor. Here the informant is allowed to describe certain ideas, beliefs, and things occurred long past (which he might have been heard from certain sources), upon the analysis of his own experience.

Generally, the data compiled by this method is not included because their lies a better chance of false description or misinterpretation of the incident occurred. But for overcoming or limiting the chance, same case is heard from different people and the data is compiled from all the phases from different people of the same locality.

Case History

Here some of the concrete cases are studied and the investigator shall take upon himself the duty of analysing or synthesising as the case may be instead of putting on the shoulder of informants. By this method, large number of cases are collected. This method helps in gathering a large number of facts concerning the social structure and other institutions.

But here is also a good chance of misinterpretation

by informants. So data are collected of all phases from different people of the same locality. There is another difficulty arises that if unit of investigation be a large one then it would be too difficult to investigate a number of people for single purpose. Generally it is of two types: (1) the person describing the case of others, (2) the person describing his own case. We refer it concrete case history.

Genealogical

In this method, the case histories are studied on the basis of a genealogy. First of all, a short genealogy of the informant is taken. In applying this method, the simplest kinship terms such as father, mother, son, daughter, brother, sister, husband and wife are generally used. The informant is asked the name of those who stand in relation to him. He is given to understand that only biological kins are to be included, but asked about how he shall address each of them and vice versa, to justify the kinship terminology factor. In the study of concrete cases, the roles of kins are often required.

After the collection of genealogy of the informant, he is asked to narrate any event in which he himself is or was directly or partially involved. He is asked to describe the happenings or roles, he has often played, thereby, he will be able to furnish a concrete cases experience by himself. In this method, the genealogy forms the basis of investigation. This method is generally known as 'Genealogical method'. Through this method, concrete cases are studied and the investigator takes upon himself the duty of analysing, instead of putting it on the shoulders of the informants.

Participant Observation

In this method, the recorder makes a functional

penetration into the system aimed to be surveyed. This participation is sometimes passive and limited to the role of spectator, but spectator is forced by circumstances to be involved in the show and be amongst the actors. The participation is often more active and can be divided into two types—(a) either the observer is external to the group to be observed, (b) or he is originally a member of the group, who endeavours to acquire the quality of an observer.

Interviews

This is a process of steady conversation, where the investigator puts certain questions to informants and the informant in turn expresses his opinion according to his desires. This technique is common to both intensive and extensive observations. In socio-anthropology interview, in depth are attempted for a deeper understanding of the opinion, attitudes and intimate the whole personality pattern of the subject.

Investigation by interview of political leaders and social elites can be a useful means of studying the social phenomena. It is important to know the differences between the opinions and attitudes of elites and the masses (in various groups and level). The interview conducted of course, remains a secret, unbiased and impersonal in nature proper to the studies of opinion. In the past few years, such studies of political leaders, social elites and establishments through the interview have been greatly developed.

Elites, leaders and prominent people are approached, because they alone can give information about certain things. These interviews are often disappointing in practice, because the political leaders do not take freely. Interview is classified according to their purposes and technical variations. Different types of interview techniques have been followed.

Repeated (Panel) Interviews

This technique was perfected by Lazarsfeld (1940), published later as the peoples' choice. Here a group of people are interviewed repeatedly at various intervals. It is based on the two ideas—(1) repetition of the same questions at regular intervals, (2) the same strata of people are interviewed throughout the enquiry, but has a limitation of distortion, where the size of sample is reduced in due course of time due to migration of people, their disinterests and non-cooperation.

Interviews in Depth

From this interview the deeper understanding can be had about opinions, attitudes and even the whole personality of the subject. Single interview in-depth is in principle where the subject in interviewed only once, although clarification can be sought in the subsequent interviews.

Focused Interviews

This technique was used by American sociologist R.K. Merton. It consists not so much by an interrogation as assisting the people to illuminate some factor or stimulus acting on them and result of this on their attitudes. This interview takes place following a particular situation common to all the people being interviewed. A film, the reading of newspapers, listening to radio programmes, etc., the aim is to study in-depth the influence of this situation, the procedure was invented to analyse the effects of communication. The contents of the basic situation are subjected to the detailed analysis, after which the hypothesis are drawn about the significance and effects of the situation.

Memoir Interviews

This procedure is for an investigator to obtain the permission from a person to interview regularly over a period of time, to question him on the events in which he has been involved. To some extent, the investigator plays the role of memoir writer. The type of person, who could be interviewed are retired politicians, directors, secretaries, local elites and notable personalities, etc.

Census Survey

Census survey in a given form gives a cross-section of a particular area on which the survey is carried on. It should be prepared according to the inherent problems. From the census data, the physical constitution as well as any cultural peculiarities comes out of any community. The cultural data against age and kin groups are observed from the census data, on the contextual observation and conversation. There is another process of data collection known as 'textual'.

Textual

Sometimes, the textual form of data collection is known as documentary data collection. History of place, previous work records, etc., are collected from the documents. There are different sources to collect such documentary data, such as—

1. *Written documents:* These are numerous and very varied such as public archives and official documents, the private archives, indirect documentation, the press and statistics.

2. *Technical Documentation:* This title used broadly to include all the subjects which man uses edifices and buildings as well as movable objects. The distinction between the technical and iconographic documentation (the latter includes drawing, engraving, picture and sculptures). These are objects such as (a) domestic, use (b) objects for defence or war such as armour, (c) instruments and tools used in productive process, (d)

religious or a medical objects, (e) political objects such as of authority and government, the dress of public servants, flags and emblems.

3. *Phonetic documentation:* A new source of sociological documentation is being created as a result of technical advances in sound recording. Linguistics are concerned with technical aspect of syntax.

Psycho-analysis

In social anthropology, man's attribution comes out of subconscious level. Presently, we find certain relationship between the overt and covert aspects in all cultural behaviour. The overt aspect of cultural behaviour is however related to the covert behaviour with inner sentiments. Socio-anthropologists understand certain behaviours of cultural level depending on the attributional analysis, as in particular caste hierarchy, affiliation of political parties, etc. M.C. Marriot used this method in the study of *Caste and Ranking in Seven Areas of North India.*

Systematic Analysis

Following the academic schemes involved in practical use, the scientific research is divided into three phases, viz., observation of the facts, formulation of the hypothesis and experimental tests of the hypotheses to transform them into laws. Towards this end, the systematic analysis is equally important as the collection of data. The elements of systematic analysis could be classified into three categories:

1. Conceptual framework of research,
2. Experimental and
3. Comparative method.

The conceptual framework implies the classification

of facts in more or less precise typology in the three levels of expression. An experiment can be defined as provoked under directed observation, one or more artificial facts, however, are introduced. The comparative method relies on comparing the data from analogous phenomena and those of differing views. Regarding the techniques, either close comparison or distant comparison modes are followed. Close comparison made between analogous types of structure is generally an institutional comparison and would remain rarely functional.

7 Anthropology in Practice

The study of anthropology is the holistic study of man. It deals with both biological and cultural aspects. It is not fruitful if the subject anthropology is limited only at the study level. There must be some implications in its study, and it is known as the applied branch of anthropology and ultimately in 1895 termed as Applied Anthropology by Brinton. Malinowski described the applied anthropology as the practical aspect of the subject.

The British colonial administrators in India took the help of anthropological knowledge for planning and smooth administration. Similarly for the administration of routine issues of the American Indians as well as those of the trust territories in the Pacifics by the U.S.A., the help of anthropological knowledge was taken.

According to Evans Pritchard, "it is the policy of colonial Government to administer people through their chiefs" (Bhowmick).

Phillip Gulliver says, "the word 'Applied' seems to mean policy-making, planning and implication and it might involve responsibility" (Bhowmick).

Forde mentions that applied anthropology must give

suggestions to apply the anthropological knowledge by the administrators for formulation of Government policies.

Nadel S.F. suggested that anthropologists should give advice in policy making. According to him while making policies, especially in land settlement and reform schemes, public health campaign, community development projects, etc., the government and administration should follow any suggestions made from the anthropologists from time to time.

Sol Tax (1951) proposed the concept of Action Anthropology. He wrote that whether applied anthropology and action anthropology are of the same variety or not depends upon one's own conception of applied anthropology and action anthropology. Bhowmick wrote that applied anthropology "presupposes a body of dependent empirical propositions developed by theoretical anthropologists, awaiting its application to particular situations, when we are asked to do so by any particular management, Government, Administrator or organisation". According to Sol Tax, these two faculties differ in concept. He wrote "if applied anthropology presupposes a body of scientific knowledge compendent empirical propositions—developed by the theoretical anthropologists and awaiting application to particular situations when we are asked to do so by management, government, administrators, or organization then action anthropology is far different ...... the action anthropologist can have no master; he works as a member of the academic community" (Sol Tax, 1968).

In fact, the action anthropology as a whole is the new knowledge developed in the mind of an anthropologist during his work in a particular situation and he feels to replace it by old knowledge, applicable in that particular situation. The anthropologist must have some theoretical knowledge.

Sol Tax opined that action anthropologists should use their knowledge for the welfare of the people without hurting their cultural norms and values using such clinical approach.

Vidyarthy (1968) had not differentiated the applied and action anthropologies. He wrote that the action and applied anthropologists could serve the human societies, who pass their ideas on acquiring from their studies. The applied and action anthropologists or the action social scientists diagnose the diseases prescribe the proper medicine by which a society will be healthy and happy. The applied and action anthropologists can give a knowledge about "their concept of culture and their tolerance of cultures" (Vidyarthy, 1968). They (the applied and action anthropologists) understand that the people value their culture, its identity and resist such changes which they think not suitable for their culture. At its operational level, they can assist a community to discover and reach its goal in a way without disturbing their cultural norms. Vidyarthy (1968) finally called them as social doctors. He opined that besides the academic field (the applied and action anthropology in India) the anthropologists should act as social doctors to help the overall administration. Either they may act as consultants to the team of administrators from outside or work jointly with them. Sometimes, a social scientist takes the responsibility to develop a society under his study. Dr. Bhowmick's work on the Lodhas of West Bengal is one such example. The action anthropologists are responsible for actions and research.

In this regard Dr. P.K. Bhowmick wrote that the applied and the action anthropologists are the right persons, who can serve the society at several levels. Initially, they can create an atmosphere of understanding between the people and the administrators. They can exactly identify the situation and such factors which may create absolute resistance in the implementation of developmental plans, as social doctors. They can serve for the benefit of people, community or nation without hurting their cultural norms and values.

The applied anthropologists beside giving suggestions for planning and development also solve the problems of public health, community development, and family planning, etc.

There are several non-governmental social welfare and developmental agencies and voluntary bodies such as Vikas Bharati in Gumla district of Chotanagpur plateau of Bihar and Ashra at Bondo hills in Mudulipada of Malkangiri district of Orissa. These organisations work for the social welfare among native tribals. In their work it will be much more helpful, if they take help and advice from the anthropologists, who have a theoretical base and also practical knowledge.

When India became free from the British colonial administration, her administrators faced several practical problems, which are the hindrances for the development of the country. The first of all is its unique caste system which differentiate people from one another with a view of high and low, purity and impurity or pollution concept of economic apartheid is dominant even today. Nextly, being a secular democratic country, where several religious groups co-exist, so there should be religious tolerance among them. There are several tribal groups who also suffer from suppression. Except these issues, India has her own problems viz., economic problems, illiteracy, superstitions, beliefs, backwardness, etc. In this situation the applied and action anthropologists should extend their hands of cooperation to the administrators and planners by giving their valuable suggestions which come out as their research results and these should be incorporated by the planners and administrators whenever they are engaged with certain developmental issues or to solve some problems.

At present action and applied anthropology got its importance with other social sciences to the planners and administrators. There are several orientation courses are available for the administrators and workers. The anthropologists are taking part in it. Vidyarthi (1968) wrote that several problems oriented research works are done for effective formulation and implementation of development programmes. There are several research institutes which are run by the State or Central Governments with the aim and objective of their studies and researches are in the field of action and applied anthropology, but these should be allowed to function at organised levels by the team of practical minded anthropologists—the SOCIAL DOCTORS.

8 Culture Change

We the anthropologists are concerned with the study of group behaviour, that is, our unit of observation is group behaviour. Again such group behaviour has two components one is overt or explicit behaviour which means the behaviour which we can directly observe that may be termed as *norms* while the other component is covert or implicit behaviour which we cannot see but can feel through empathy that is called value of such behaviour. When changes are occurred in the former level it is known as social change while changes are found both in norms and its value level it is called as culture change.

Change is simply variability in culture and behaviour over time. 'Culture change' generally refers not to the short term dynamics of particular cultures but to large scale alterations in the organisation and operation of a society. According to Fred Plog and Daniel G. Bates (1976), the major changes are likely to be the accumulated product of much smaller changes occurring over a period of years. "Culture is ever changing. Since cultures consists of learned patterns of behaviour and belief, cultural traits can be unlearned and learned anew as human needs to change. Thus, no specific cultural pattern remains impervious to change, just as no specific item of learning is necessarily immortal" (Ember and Ember, 1977). Most of us are highly aware that 'times have changed' and along with this people's way of life and their behaviour pattern. We being cultural anthropologists also try to understand how and why the changes have took place and it's consequences effect on the society.

There are various factors which are responsible for socio-cultural change in a society. Internal factors such as new invention may lead to an increased food supply, population growth or external factors like conquest, war or revolt, education, set up and as well as rise of industrial units, rise of communication facilities, migration, contact between two societies and even adaptation of a culture to its environment (Steward, 1955), etc.

According to E.Z. Vogt (1960) culture change may be summarised in four basic questions—

(i) What are the internal or external factors that generate shifts in rates and types of culture change?

(ii) What are the process by which culture change takes place?

(iii) What models and methods are now available for the study of culture change?

(iv) How is the concept of culture change related to the closely associated phenomena of diffusion, innovation, evolution, acculturation and nativism?

Socio-cultural change in India indicates profound effects on economic change. The effect of the new economic order upon the way of life of Indian society is clearly evidenced in industry. The reason behind such are induction of modern technology like radio, cable

TV, video cassettes, satellite network, pager, cellular telephone and various kinds of industrial set ups and overall globalisation of new open economic policy. Technology produces social inventions and also social change. Automobiles and electricity are now spreading industry almost everywhere. All these are responsible for changing scenario of socio-cultural life of human beings. Bottomore (1962) has noted that "two elements have played a decisive part in bringing about social change in India, first, western science and technology and secondly, social planning. ...... The introduction of capitalist industry brought about changes in the property system and in the division of labour and gave rise to new social strata and classes which played an important part in the political development in India".

Culture change can be studied as it occurs over long time spans and in the microscopic sense, as it occurs in short periods of time. In regard to microscopic models the work of White (1949) and Childe (1951) may be taken as example for the study of cultural evolution. White's most significant proposition is that technological development expressed in terms of man's control over energy underlies social changes and cultural achievements. Childe is especially noted for his formulation of neolithic revolution which means development of cultures from food gathering societies to settled agricultural food producing societies, in early human history. Another model which involves social and cultural changes over prolonged time spans is the contribution of Redfield (1942) when he studied folk and urban society and tried to show an continuum between the two as well as culture change. While among microscopic models the contribution of Murdock (1949) and Leach (1954) are focussed upon changing and cultural systems. Murdock is mainly concerned with changes in social organisation. He proposes that change in social system regularly begins with a modification of rule of residence and other changes in kinship structure and terminology follow in predictable order, while Leach utilizes "oscillation model" among Kachin society where is a regular oscillation between two polar types with different political value systems.

Infact, to understand socio-culture change a controlled group must be identified for understanding change in synchronic level and when such changes are observed through prolonged time spans that is through diachronic level then the evidences of history and genealogy are essential.

In short, with the advent of agriculture, food supply becomes certain incomparison to earlier feature of uncertainty in food through hunting. Thus, agriculture brought a change in the distribution of population in villages. Again with the introduction of industry in the subsistence sector, the monetary economy is gaining importance and as a result a rapid changes are observed in socio-cultural way of life of the people. Thus, industrialisation has revolutionised the socio-economic and socio-cultural life of the people.

Anthropologists of nineteenth century and twentieth century first became interested in culture change as a result of contact with peoples who were altogether different from the western cultures with which they were accustomed. This explanation for the differences were ultimately gave birth the theory of evolution. More recently, interest has centered upon the process of modernization in the third world countries where induction of industrial economy and it's value system, migration of people and adaptation of western way of life have led a major cultural change.

BIBLIOGRAPHY

Ardener, E., 1970, *Social Anthropology and Language.*

Basham, A.L. (ed.), 1984, *A Cultural History of India* (2nd Impression) Delhi : Oxford University Press.

Banerjee, S., 1981, *Impact of Industrialisation on the tribal population of Jharia—Ranigunge Coal Field Area,* Calcutta : Anthropological Survey of India.

Beals, R.L. and H. Hoijer (2nd edition) 1959, *An Introduction to Anthropology,* New York : The Macmillan & Co.

Becker, H. and A. Boskoff 1957, *Modern Sociological Theory: In Continuity and Change,* U.S.A. Rinehart and Winston Hott.

Bhowmick, P.K., *Role of Applied Anthropology in Administration and Planning for Social Development.*

Bose, N.K., 1948, a. *Hindu Samajer Garan* (in Bengali), Calcutta : Viswa Bharati Granthalay.

———, 1951, b. "Caste System in India", *Man in India*, Vol. XXXI.

———, 1953, c. *Cultural Anthropology and other Essay*, Calcutta : Indian Associated Publishing Co. Ltd.

———, 1961, d. *Cultural Anthropology*, Calcutta : Asia Publishing House.

Bottomore, T.B., 1971, *Sociology*, Bombay : George Allen and Unwin (India) Pvt. Ltd.

Brown, W.N.,1986, *Man in the Universe : Some Continuities in Indian Thought*, Berkeley and Los Angeles : University of California Press.

Childe, V.G., 1951, *Social Evolution*, London and New York : Copyright by H. Schuman.

Cohn, B.S., 1971, *India : Social Anthropology of a Civilization*, U.S.A., Prentice Hall.

Comte, A., 1893, *The Positive Philosophy*, London.

Das, A. and S. Banerjee, 1962, *Impact of Industrialisation on the life of the tribals of West Bengal*, Calcutta: Tribal Welfare Department,

Govt. of West Bengal, Bulletin of Cultural Research Institute, Special Series, No.1.

Dasgupta, P.K., 1964, a. "Impact of Industrialisation on the tribal life", in *Bulletin of the Anthropological Survey of India*, 13: 85-106.

——, 1972, b. *Impact of industrialisation on a tribe in south Bihar*, Calcutta : Anthropological Survey of India.

Dasgupta, Samira, 1986,a "Tribal Women Labourers in Construction Industry", *Human Science*, Vol. 25, No.1.

——, 1995, b. *In Search of Alternatives : Tribal Women in Desert Scenario*, Delhi : Gyan Publishing House.

Dube, S.C., 1958, *India's changing village*, Ithaca, New York : Cornell University Press.

Durkheim, E., 1938, *The Rules of Sociological Method*, Chicago : The University of Chicago Press.

Duverger, M., 1961, *Introduction to Methods of Social Sciences*, London : George Allen and Unwin.

Elkin, A.P., 1950, "The Complexity of Social Organisation in Arnhem-land" *South-western Jour-*

nal of Anthropology, Vol. 6, pp. 6-20 (ed.).

Evans-Pritchard, E.E., 1951 — *Social Anthropology* New York: Free Press

Firth, Raymond, 1951, a. — *Elements of Social Organisation*, London: Watts and Co.

———, 1954, b. — "Presidential Address", in *Journal of Royal Anthropological Institute*, Vol. 84.

Forde, G.D., 1979, (reprinted) — *Habitat, Economy and Society*, London: Methuen & Co. Ltd.

Fox, Robin, 1975, — "Primitive Kin and Human Kinship", in *Bio Social Anthropology* (ed). Robin Fox, London : Malaby Press.

Frazer, J.D., 1910, — *Totemism and Exogamy*, Vol. I, London : Macmillan & Co. Ltd.

Freud, Sigmund, 1931, — *Totem and Taboo*, New York: New Republic, Inc.

Geertz, Clifford, 1963, a. — *Agricultural Involution*, London: University of California Press.

———, 1973, b. — *The Interpretation of Cultures*, New York : Basic Books.

Ginsberg, M., 1934, a. — *Sociology*, London : Oxford University Press.

Ginsberg, M. 1957, b. *Essays in Sociology and Social Philosophy*, London.

Goodenough, Ward H., 1956, "Componential Analysis and Study of Meaning", *Language*, Vol. 32, pp.195-216.

Haddon, A.C., 1934, *History of Anthropology*, London : Watts & Co.

Harris, Marrin, 1966, "The Cultural Ecology of India's Sacred Cattle", *Current Anthropology*, No. 7: pp. 51-59.

Herskovits, M.J., 1948, a. *Man and His Works*, New York : Alfred Knopf.

———, 1954, b. "Some problems of method in ethnography", in *Method and Perspective in Anthropology*, ed. R.F. Spencer, Minneapolis : University of Minnesota Press.

———, 1955, c. *Cultural Anthropology*, An abridged Revision of Man and his work, New York : Alfred A. Knopf.

Hobhouse, L.T., 1915, a. *Morals in Evolution* (Third Edition).

———, 1924, b. *Social Development—Its Nature and Conditions*, London : George Allen and Unwin Ltd.

Hoslitz, B.F., 1963, "Main concepts in the

analysis of the social implications of technological change", in *Industrialisation and Society*, eds., B.F. Hoslitz and W.E. Moore, UNESCO : Mouton.

Hymes, D.H., 1963, *Objectives and Concepts of Linguistic Anthropology.*

Karve, Irawati, 1953, a. *Kinship Organisation in India*, Poona : Deccan College, Post Graduate and Research Institute.

———, 1977, b. *Hindu Society—An Interpretation* (3rd edition), Bombay: Deshmukh Prakashan.

Kluckhohn, Clyde and William Kelly, 1945, 'The Concept of Culture' in *The Science of Man in the World Crisis* (ed). by R. Linton, New York : Coloumbia University Press.

Kluckhohn, Clyde, 1953, "Universal Categories of Culture", in *Anthropology Today* (ed.) by A.L. Kroeber, Chicago : University of Chicago Press.

Kroeber, A.L., 1909, a. "Classificatory System of Relationship", *The Journal of the Royal Anthropological Institute of Great Britain and Ireland*, Vol. 30, pp.77-85.

———, 1931, b. "The Culture-area and Age-area Concepts of Clark

Wissler", in *Methods in Social Sciences*, S. Rice (ed.), Chicago : Chicago University Press.

———, 1944, c. *Configuration of Culture Growth*, Berkeley and Los Angeles : University of California Press.

———, 1948, d. *Anthropology : Race, Language, Culture, Psychology, Pre-history*, New York : Harcourt, Brace and Co. (Revised Edition).

Kroeber, A.L. and Clyde Kluckhohn, 1952, "Culture : A Critical Review of Concepts and Definitions", *Papers of the Peabody Museum of American Archaeology and Ethnology*, Vol. XLVII, No.1, p.3. (Harvard University).

Lambert, Richard, D., 1963, *Workers, Factories and Social Change in India*, Poona: Asia Publishing House.

Leach, E.R., 1961, *Rethinking Anthropology.*

Levy-Strauss, Claude, 1956, *Structural Anthropology*, New York.

Linton, R., 1947, *The Cultural Background of Personality*, London : Routledge and Kegan Paul Ltd.

Lounsbury, Floyd G., "A Semantic Analysis of the

1956, Pawnee Kinship Usage", *Language*, Vol. 32, pp. 158-94.

Lowie, R.H., 1920, a. *Primitive Society*, New York: Boni and Liveright.

———, 1929, b. "Relationship Terms", in *the Encyclopaedia Britanica*, 14th edition, London : pp. 84-89.

———, 1937, c. *The History of Ethnological Theory*, New York : Farrar and Rinehart.

———, 1950, d. *Social Organisation*, London: Routledge and Kegan Paul.

Majumdar, R.C., 1977, *Hindu Sabhyata Samaskritier Karma Vikash* (in Bengali) Calcutta : University of Calcutta.

Marcus, E. George and Michael M.J. Fischer, 1986, *Anthropology as Cultural Critique : An Experimental Moment in the Human Sciences*, Chicago and London : The University of Chicago Press.

Marriott, Mckim, 1955, "Little Communities in an Indigenous Civilization", *Village India*, Mckim Marriott, ed. Chicago : University of Chicago Press.

Marriott, Mckim and B.S. Cohn, 1958, "Network and Centres in Integration of Indian

Civilization", *Journal of Social Research*, Vol.1, No.1.

Marriott, Mckim, 1959, "Interaction and Attributional Theories of Caste, Ranking", *Man in India*, Vol.39, No.2, pp. 92-107.

Marriott, M. (ed.), 1966, *Village India : Studies in the Little Community* (6th Impression), Chicago : University of Chicago Press.

Mayer, A.C., 1960, *Caste and Kinship in Central India : A Village and its Region*, London : Routledge and Kegan Paul (Indian Edition : Allied Publishers Pvt. Ltd.).

Moore, W.E., 1963, *Social Change*, New Jersey: Prentice Hall.

Morgan, L.H., 1877, *Ancient Society*, New York: World Publishing Society.

Mukherjee, Bhabananda, 1981, *Structure and Kinship in Tribal India*, Calcutta : Minerva Associates (Publication) Pvt. Ltd.

Muller, M., 1861, Lectures on Science of Language, Biographics of words and the Home of the Aryans, 1889.

Murdock, G.P., 1949, a. *Social Structure*, New York : Collier Macmillan.

Murdock, George, P., 1955, b. "Changing Emphasis in Social Structure", *South Western Journal of Anthropology*, Vol.II, pp. 361-70.

Murdock, George, P., 1957, c. *World Ethnographic Sample.*

Nadel, S.F., 1957, *The Theory of Social Structure,* London : Cohen and West.

Nair, Kusum, 1961, *Blossoms in the Dust*, London : Gerald Duck Worth & Co. Ltd.

Nash, Manning, 1958, *Machine Age Maya : The Industrialization of a Guatemalan Community*, Illinois, The Free Press of Glen Co. Mem. 87. The American Anthropological Association.

Nikkam, N.A., 1967, *Some Aspects of Indian Culture: A Philosophical Interpretation*, Simla : Indian Institute of Advance Study.

Orans, Martin, 1965, *The Santal : A Tribe in Search of Great Tradition,* Detroit : Wayne State University Press.

Orlove, Benjamin S., 1980, "Ecological Anthropology" in *Annual Rev. Anthropology*, 9 : 234-73.

Parson, T., 1954, *Social System*, London : Tavistock Publication.

Radcliffe Brown, 1952, *Structure and Function in Primitive Society*, London : Cohen and West Ltd.

Radha Krishan, S., 1954, *Hindu View of Life* (9th Impression), London : Allen and Unwin.

Rambo, A. Terry, 1983, "Conceptual Approaches to Human Ecology", Research Report, No.14, Honolulu, Hawaii, East-west Environment and Policy Institute.

Rappaport, Roy A., 1968, a. *Pigs for the Ancestors*, New Haven, Conn : Yale University Press.

———, 1969, b. "Ritual Regulations of Environmental Relations among a New Guinea People", in *Environment and Cultural Behaviour*, (ed.) A.P. Vayda, New York : The Natural History Press.

Redfield, Robert, 1941, a. *The Folk Culture of Yucatan*, Chicago : Chicago University Press.

———, 1947, b. "The Folk Society", *American Journal of Sociology*, Vol. 52, No. 4, pp. 293-308.

———, 1955, c. *The Little Community*, Chicago: Chicago University Press.

Redfield, Robert, 1956, d. *Peasant Society and Culture: An Anthropological Approach to Civilization*, Chicago: Chicago University Press.

Redfield, Robert and Milton B. Singer, 1954, "The Cultural Role of Cities" *Economic Development and Culture Change*, Vol. 8, No.1, pp. 53-73 (Chicago).

Renou, L. (ed.), 1961, *Hinduism*, London : Prentice Hall International.

Sahlins, M.D., 1964, "Culture and Environment: The Study of Cultural Ecology", in *Horizons of Anthropology*, (ed.), Sol Tax, London : Allen and Unwin Ltd.

Saraswati, B.N., 1970, a. *Contribution to the Study of Indian Civilisation*, Karnataka: Dharwar University.

——, 1978, b. "Sacred Complexes in Indian Cultural Traditions", in *Eastern Anthropologists*, Vol. 31, No.1.

Sarkar, Amitabha, 1988,a. "Impact of industrialization among the Dhodias of Gujarat", *Human Science*, Vol. 37, No. 3.

——,1993, *Dhodia : Industrialisation and change in a Primitive Community*, New Delhi : Gyan Publishing House.

Sarma, Gopala, 1975, *The Methodology of Anthropological Comparisons: An Analysis of Comparative Methods in Social and Cultural Anthropology*, Arizona : The University of Arizona Press.

Sayce, A.H., 1887, *Science of Languages.*

Schneider, David, M. 1968, *American Kinship : A Cultural Account*, New Jersey, Prentice Hall, Inc.

Semple, E.C., 1911, *Influences of Geographic Environment : On the Basis of Ratzel's System of Anthropo-Geography*, New York : Henry Hott.

Simmel, G., 1902, "The number of members as determining the social forms of the groups", *American Journal of Society*, Vol. VIII.

Singer, Milton, 1958, *Traditional India: Structure and Change*, Philadelphia : American Folklore Society.

Singer, Milton, 1972, *When a Great Tradition Modernises; An Anthropological Approach to Indian Civilization*, Delhi : Vikas Publishing House.

Spencer, H., 1872, *Study of Sociology*, Kanpur: Kitab Ghar (Indian Edition).

——, 1876, *Evolution of Society*,

Chicago: Chicago University Press.

Spier, L., 1925, *The Distribution of Kinship System in North America,* University of Washington, Publication in Anthropology; 75-76.

Steward, J.H., 1955, a. *Theory of Culture Change,* Urbana : University of Illinois Press.

———, 1968, b. "Cultural Ecology", in *International Encyclopaedia of Social Sciences,* Vol.14, pp. 337-44.

Tax, S., 1968, "Action Anthropology", in *Applied Anthropology in India,* (pp. 31-41), (ed.) L.P. Vidyarthi, Allahabad: Kitab Mahal.

Toynbee, A.J., 1947, *A Study of History* (abridgement of Vols. I-VI) New York : Oxford University Press.

Tylor, E.B., 1871, *Primitive Culture : Researches into the Development of Mythology, Philosophy, Religion, Language, Art and Custom,* London : John Murray.

Vayda, Andrew, P., 1968, "Economic Systems in Ecological Perspective : The Case of the North-west coast", in *Readings in*

Anthropology, Vol. II (ed.) Fried. H. Morton, New York: Thomas Y. Crowell Company.

Vidyarthi, L.P., 1968, "Introduction", *Applied Anthropology in India*, (ed.) L.P. Vidyarthi, Allahabad : Kitab Mahal.

———, 1970, *Socio-Cultural Implications of Industrialisation in India: A Case Study of Tribal Bihar*, New Delhi, Delite Press.

Weber, Max, 1930, a. *Protestant ethics and the spirit of capitalism*, London: George Allen and Unwin (Translated by Talcott Parson).

———, 1947, b. *The Theory of Social and Economic Organisation*, (A.M. Henderson and Talcott Parson, Trans.), New York: Oxford University Press.

———, 1949, c. *On the Methodology of Social Sciences*, (E.A. Shils and H.D. Finch, trans.), New York : The Free Press of Glencoe.

Westermarck, E.A., 1921, *The History of Human Marriage.*

White, A.L., 1959, *The Evolution of Culture: The*

Development of Civilization to the Fall of Rome, London: Mc-Grew Hill Company.

Wissler, Clark, 1929, *An Introduction to Social Anthropology*, New York : Henry Holt and Co.

Index